Invent Business Opportunities No One Else Can Imagine

Invent Business Opportunities No One Else Can Imagine

Trendsetting companies
disarm their competition
and
astound their customers.
Will you be one of them?

by Art Turock

CA·REER
PRESS
Franklin Lakes, NJ

INVENT BUSINESS OPPORTUNITIES NO ONE ELSE CAN IMAGINE
Edited by Nicole DeFelice
Typeset by John J. O'Sullivan
Cover design by Greg Wilkin
Printed in the U.S.A. by Book-mart Press

To order this title, please call toll-free 1-800-CAREER-1 (NJ and Canada: 201-848-0310) to order using VISA or MasterCard, or for further information on books from Career Press.

CAREER
PRESS

The Career Press, Inc., 3 Tice Road, PO Box 687,
Franklin Lakes, NJ 07417
www.careerpress.com

Library of Congress Cataloging-in-Publication Data

Turock, Art, 1950-
    Invent business opportunities no one else can imagine / by Art Turock.
      p. cm.
    Includes index.
    ISBN 1-56414-578-6
              1. Business planning. 2. Strategic planning. I. Title.

HD30.28 .T825 2001
658.4'012--dc21   200135363

Acknowledgments

Randy Howatt, who first saw the value of my ideas and without whose encouragement, this book would never have been written. When a leader has earned membership in Young Presidents' Organization and World Presidents' Organization, his opinion carries clout.

My team of book reviewers, who gave generously of their time and their expertise in providing incredibly helpful feedback. Thanks to Bob Swellie of American Greetings, Jack Kopnisky, President of Key Bank, Andy Eckert of Storecast Merchandising Corporation, Dr. Linne Bourget of the Institute of Transformational Leadership, Bob Peters, Managing Partner with KPMG, Robert Holmes, CEO of Harbor Properties, Bruce Pettet, CEO of TARE7, and Karen Holt, Founder of Colores.

Selma Turock, my mother, who instilled the incredible gift of never settling for less than what I truly desire in life.

Haley Ashland, my wife and best friend, who is the constant stimulus for new learning in our business and our relationship.

Mary Lynne Hanley, of Maystar Communications, who in a memorable three week period gave incredible passion, energy, and impeccable judgment in the transformative editing of my original manuscript.

Dr. Henriette Klauser of Writing Resources, who offered exceptional savvy and skill in the preparation of my book proposal and in connecting with my excellent literary agent, Jane Dystel.

Contents

Chapter

1

Gaining a Sustainable Advantage

Chapter

1

Gaining a Sustainable Advantage

"Two roads diverged in a wood, and I—
I took the one less traveled by,
And that has made all the difference."
—from the poem "The Road Not Taken" by Robert Frost

Most of us have no idea of the powerful influence the past exerts on our choices and actions today. **No idea.** Not even close.

Why have titans such as IBM, Sears, AT&T, and General Motors "hit a wall" somewhere along the marathon of shaping their business destiny? Could it be that winning companies are now threatened by a hidden disadvantage that isn't shared by their middling competitors?

The disadvantage is not complacency. Successful business leaders are already alert to the threat of complacency. No, they are plagued by a disadvantage that defies detection because it is imbedded within the best practices that were immensely effective in the past—their winning formula.

What are the challenges in sustaining a competitive advantage?

How can successful companies lose with a winning formula? Don't they have ample evidence of success—solid sales, market share, profitability, quality measures, and customer satisfaction data? They know what works. Surely the numbers don't lie.

When business is on a roll, the logical strategy is to repeat the winning formula. When results plateau or nosedive, it only seems rational to push the winning formula harder and harder. But the shelf life of winning formulas gets shorter and shorter. The rules of competition change. Now time-honored techniques may yield only "antiquated" excellence—high quality products and services that the marketplace no longer prizes. The value offering is excellent—for yesterday's customer.

Will doing more of what brought you success in the past bring about the future you desire? In growing numbers, senior executives are realizing a painful truth—no company, regardless of size, wealth, reputation, or market share, can rely on doing what worked in the past. Sustained success now demands the creation of new sources of competitive advantage. It requires innovation.

Recent history offers compelling evidence of the power of innovation in achieving sustainable advantage. Between 1986 and 1996, only 17 members of the Fortune 1000 grew their total shareholder returns by 35 percent or more per year. This superstar list includes Amgen, Conseco, Harley-Davidson, Home Depot, Nike, Oracle and Pacificare Health Systems. Far beyond product and service upgrades, these wealth creators focused on inventing new industries or remaking the rules of competition in their existing markets. Sustainable competitive advantage goes to companies that discover opportunities no one else—neither their customers nor their competitors—can imagine.

So what is the barrier? If we know we need to innovate, why aren't more companies doing it? Why does nearly every industry have only a handful of trailblazers, while the rest plod along in the same ruts they've plowed for decades?

The Fatal Assumption

An often hidden assumption underlies most business strategies, one that feeds on time-honored faith in the eternal efficacy of a winning formula. It's rarely easy to recognize, especially when a business is on a profit-making roll. But I must expose this shadowy supposition for what it actually is: an absolutely fatal assumption.

Here's how many businesses express this Fatal Assumption: *The strategies that brought us success in the past will inevitably continue to work in the future, as long as we just implement them better and/or with greater effort.*

Why is this assumption is fatal? Because it just doesn't fit today's ever-changing business environment.

Many have difficulty acknowledging the Fatal Assumption, especially when a business is still profitable. Indeed, the brave souls that dare openly to wonder whether the winning formula is still working are few and far between.

Even as the pace of change peaks in most industries, most of us find it easier, and often safer, to blame a variety of "culprits," or indulge in denial and wishful thinking—anything but confront the demise of our winning formula.

We yearn for the golden days when we could milk the cash cow product for years, instead of months, without having to commit to any sort of change...or even *talk* about changing anything.

We watch e-commerce take hold in other industries and hope our industry will somehow get by unscathed.

Even though we keep raising our performance standards, our competitors are also doing such high quality work that customers can scarcely differentiate.

We maintain our traditional low-price strategy even as new mega-giant competitors use their economies of scale to whittle down prices to a level we can't afford to match.

We hold off from investing in a promising innovation because none of our competitors has figured out how to do it profitably, and we don't dare go first.

Does any of this sound familiar? When you are at a strategic cross-roads, it is not easy to confront the need for innovation and change. It is, indeed, "the road less traveled."

The dangerous compromise

Why is there such reluctance to embrace the obvious solution—innovation? Most business leaders are not convinced they have to pursue bold innovation to the degree that is required today. They don't recognize the increasing demand for original thinking that is required just to keep pace, let alone lead a market. Consequently, insufficient effort is made to develop the strategies and organizational culture where innovation can flourish. Ultimately, the Fatal Assumption produces a dangerous compromise—settling for short-term profitability instead of playing for a sustainable competitive advantage.

We are witnessing a fundamental divergence in the pathway to competitive advantage. Between 1925 and 1985, the business environment was tranquil compared to today's turbulence. In the book, *Marketing Warfare,* strategists Al Ries and Jack Trout cite a study of leading brands (e.g., Ivory in soap, Campbell in soup, Coca-Cola in soft drinks) in 25 different industries. Twenty of the 25 market leaders in 1925 were still on top 60 years later.

During this period, the Fatal Assumption reflected business realities. Industry boundaries remained intact. Competitors were well known and came from within one's own industry, rarely from other industries. Market leaders set the rules and used their unfair advantages to ward off, even destroy, competition. Product innovation was an advantage that took years for a competitor to emulate. The supply channel of manufacturers, wholesalers, and distributors had well-defined and intact roles. Customers were less knowledgeable, less demanding, and less diverse in their needs than they are today. There was no Internet. In such a relatively tranquil market, strategy tweaking and incremental change were sufficient to stay ahead. Strategic makeover was overkill.

Those pre-1985 market conditions are gone, replaced by globalization, computerization, consolidation, and deregulation. As they confront change and the need for a new strategy, companies choose one of two distinct models.

Replicator companies retain their faith in the Fatal Assumption. Consequently, they have excessive reverence for their winning formula. Rather than initiate bold innovation, replicators focus on improving quality, exerting more vigorous effort, or making slight adjustments to their basic strategic moves.

Casting aside the Fatal Assumption, trendsetter companies analyze the continuing effectiveness of even their most sacred winning formulas. Trendsetters realize their talent for original thinking is a formidable advantage when used to produce business opportunities that no one else could imagine.

Although the rest of this book will expand on how to develop the winning ways of trendsetters, let's spend a little more time now comparing the characteristics of replicators and trendsetters.

Replicators and Trendsetters

Replicators come in two types: conformists and copycats. Conformists enshrine themselves in a profitable niche with a simple game plan:

Stick with the familiar core business, ask customers what they want, make requested improvements. The conformists' motto is: "continuous improvement is as good as we need to be."

Copycats are those "me-too" companies whose strategy is simply to keep pace with their competition's emerging innovations. Essentially, if a competitor's innovation succeeds, copycats soon adopt it.

The common threat in both breeds of replicators is that neither is doing any thinking for themselves. Either the strategy is inherited from the previous senior management team and is adopted with minor tweaking, or it is copied from a hot competitor's strategic moves. The lack of original thinking is evident in the resulting strategy: replicators create a future that amounts to bringing the past forward.

The pursuit of entrepreneurial freedom

In contrast, trendsetters design strategies that depend on original thinking.

One group of trendsetters—"innovation catalysts"—conceive new products, services, and business models. Their goal is to reap the sales growth, profitability and brand equity benefits that come from being first to market.

The second type of trendsetters—"best of the best"—are happy to let others be first, but eventually they perfect the innovation better than its originator. "Best of the best" trendsetters capitalize on their superior ability to see the full implications of a primitive but promising idea and their greater capacity for introducing innovation to the marketplace.

Both trendsetter strategies depend on highly original strategic thinking. As a by-product, customers receive products and services they've never before experienced, or have never thought to request. Trendsetters literally create new marketplace demand, and accelerate the emergence of an unprecedented future. Their visions become our realities: Personal computers on every office desktop, plastic credit cards replacing paper money, and wireless telecommunications all began in the minds of industry trendsetters and eventually changed the world as we know it. Trendsetters demonstrate independent thinking and use courageous resolve to pursue unscripted strategic paths.

Because the Fatal Assumption doesn't influence trendsetters, they are free to exercise a larger range of choices in their quality of thinking and their actions. I call this expanded capacity for choosing "entrepreneurial freedom." An entrepreneur is anyone that manages and assumes the risks of doing business. The concept can apply to both business owners and employees who feel a sense of ownership for their slice of the business. The following distinctions between replicators and trendsetters reveal their respective ranges of entrepreneurial freedom.

Replicators	Trendsetters
Prefer predictability	Favor unpredictability that invites imagination.
Avoid the risk of change	Believe the greatest risk is waiting until circumstances force change.
Are managers who wish to preserve the past	Are leaders who shape the future.
Look for evidence that something works, and fear making mistakes	Treat mistakes as an integral part of the experimentation necessary for doing anything original.
React to trends.	Anticipate trends and accelerate them.
Accept commoditization as inevitable.	Seek to become copy-resistant.
Are concerned about mature markets.	Realize market maturity disappears when new value is introduced.
Look for agreement and view deviation as dangerous.	Do what industry incumbents consider "going too far" and see conformity as dangerous.
Base business strategy on giving customers what they request.	Give customers what they had never thought of asking for.
Develop strategies based on the dictates of prevailing circumstances.	Reshape circumstances to propel their desired future.
Rely on proven answers.	Raise provocative questions that accelerate learning.

Trendsetters can exercise the replicator choices when market conditions dictate slow and steady change. But when there is a chance to leapfrog the competition, trendsetters have the power to make additional choices that aren't available to replicators.

The advantage of focusing on latent needs

Let's examine the pattern in which a trendsetter's entrepreneurial freedom produces a sustainable advantage. The heart of the trendsetters' advantage is their extraordinary customer focus. While replicators are content to ask customers what they want and give it to them, they achieve lackluster results. Why? Lacking a Jules Verne-like imagination, customers rarely dream up novel needs. At best, they are content with minor adjustments to existing products and services.

Rather than listening to customers' direct requests, trendsetters probe for latent needs that customers can't express or can't even imagine being met.

The ability to recognize and find solutions to latent needs is the most powerful weapon in the trendsetter's strategic armory—as revealed in the unexpectedly innovative strategy of USAA Insurance during the Desert Storm war.

Even McDonald's and Coca Cola would envy USAA Insurance's astonishing share of its market—94 percent. How do they do it? They regulary break the established insurance underwriting rules and meet the latent needs of their primary policyholders—military personnel and their families.

During Desert Storm, USAA Insurance offered what no other insurance company in the country was willing to provide. They *boosted* the life insurance coverage of troops heading into a combat zone in Iraq, while retaining the standard rate. New policy holders were accepted even after they were called to ship overseas.

There's more. USAA set up a hotline so if a policyholder was killed, the claimant could make a single phone call for help with the family's life insurance, property insurance, bank accounts, and investment management.

The USAA Insurance offer reflected enormous "generosity." Even though the company managed its overall risk by placing a cap on how much life insurance the combatants could buy—$25,000 coverage for lieutenants and captains, $50,000 for officers ranked major or above—its break with industry precedents astounded customers and left its competitors in the dust. Given the firm's extraordinary support for its active-duty customers, it is not surprising that USAA attracted the loyalty of 94 percent of its market segment. That type of sterling reputation is the source of sustainable competitive advantage.

The seven big ideas

Based on my 19 years of observing Fortune 500 businesses and mom 'n' pop operations, I believe that trendsetters' choices and actions, like those of USAA Insurance, are the product of an atypical set of ideas they hold about four factors: strategy, innovative thinking, leadership and organizational culture. I have summarized these into seven "Big Ideas."

Businesses that ignore the Big Ideas gradually succumb to the increasing influence of the Fatal Assumption and eventually spiral into decline.

Businesses that master the Big Ideas tap into latent needs and invent opportunities that result in enormous sales growth.

What qualifies an idea as "BIG?" A Big Idea offers an extraordinary perspective for interpreting familiar circumstances. Instead of accepting a few conventional solutions to a dilemma, a fresh perspective allows new possibilities to emerge, potential solutions that are all but invisible to most others. Ultimately, each Big Idea brings greater access to the illusive ingredient that propels trendsetters—their unique way of sizing up business challenges and opportunities.

The purpose of the Seven Big Ideas on page 19 is to weaken the control exerted by the Fatal Assumption and to restore each business to its full capacity for entrepreneurial freedom.

Each of the next seven chapters is a detailed discussion of these Big Ideas.

Are you ready to innovate?

Trendsetters express the transcendent nature of business. They are not mainly motivated by "show-me-the-money" greed or a "just-enough-to-earn-a-living" mentality. In my experience, true innovators embark on a daring journey to manifest their dreams. Along the way, they teach valuable lessons

---

- **Big Idea #1**: Today's strategic priorities must focus on innovating for the future rather than improving on the past.
- **Big Idea #2**: Be the only one that does what you do.
- **Big Idea #3**: Give customers what they need but might never even think to ask for.
- **Big Idea #4**: Observe the familiar with fresh eyes.
- **Big Idea #5**: Questions are the seeds of innovation.
- **Big Idea #6**: An organization's trendsetting capacity is a reflection of its leader's beliefs.
- **Big Idea #7**: Develop a culture that aligns employee behavior with the organization's innovative strategy.

---

to their employees who have the privilege of participating in such an invigorating environment. Trendsetting organizations are learning laboratories infused by the force of entrepreneurial freedom.

Invent Business Opportunities No One Else Can Imagine is, first and foremost, a book about increasing freedom of choice. This freedom of choice offers business owners and corporate CEOs the opportunity and responsibility to conceive their own business strategies. Additionally, it encourages employees to share customer insights and propose promising projects in partnership with their company's strategists.

While all organizations have the freedom to shape their own destiny, every organizational leader with bold aspirations must answer these questions: Are we taking advantage of the entrepreneurial freedom that's here for the taking? Are we willing to seize its power or will we settle for squandering it?

Chapter

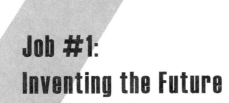

2

Job #1:
Inventing the Future

Chapter

2

Job #1:
Inventing the Future

"To really help the organization meet today's business requirements and prepare for tomorrow's, vision must be pragmatically and unabashedly bifocal: it must simultaneously paint a picture of the opportunities today and the 'best bets' of tomorrow, and, when push comes to shove, it must prioritize the latter."

—Oren Harari, *Leapfrogging the Competition*

Conventional thinking suggests that the upper limits of achievement are determined by how effectively we build on the past. But this is a notion that supports the Fatal Assumption.

Almost everything in our conditioning argues that living powerfully is founded on past experience, education, upbringing, developed skills, successes, and failures. Businesses build on established assets such as past strategies, brand equity, resources, market share, talent, company culture, even the quality of teamwork.

How do you manage for the short-term, while also innovating for the future?

I am proposing that the unique capacity for trendsetting innovation works in the opposite way.

What if our lives in the present were not merely some variation of building on the past?

What if we were not limited to simply doing more of the same, better or harder?

Is it possible to envision a future that is not limited by our history, one in which our actions bring about changes that could not be predicted?

Isn't the power to invent the future essential for creating business opportunities no one else can imagine?

Big Idea #1 represents a shift in priorities on a scale that is rarely witnessed in most companies. The shift rejects the Fatal Assumption in favor of imagining a desired future and mobilizing efforts to make it a reality.

Big Idea # 1: Today's strategic priorities must focus on innovating for the future rather than improving on the past.

This chapter will enable you to capitalize on the power that comes in mastering this concept. We'll start by clarifying common misconceptions about what inventing the future entails. Later, we will examine three methods used by trendsetters to deliver today's results, while simultaneously reinventing their businesses for the future.

The future is a cat burglar

"We think of the future as a soon-to-be-occupied home that will come to us unburdened by inheritance taxes, mortgage or the like," wrote futurist Ryan Mathews in *Progressive Grocer*. "The truth is that the future slips into our lives like a cat burglar—unknown, hiding in the shadows of the extended present, lying undetected until its presence finally comes to define the very parameters of our existence."

Like cat burglars, emerging market trends and competitive strategies make inroads today, while laying the groundwork for an even larger impact tomorrow. Rather than suddenly appearing as our reality at some distant time, the future is subtly taking hold now. The business owner who sleeps peacefully through the night is likely to wake up and find the jewels missing. Another business has stolen his prized customers. Unfortunately, the business owner's tranquil slumber came from erroneous faith in the Fatal Assumption. Relying on outdated winning formulas amounts to leaving the windows open so the cat burglar can clean out the house.

But what if a company was alert to encroaching cat burglars and could capitalize on emerging changes? That company would be orchestrating its priorities by focusing greater attention on inventing the future rather than protecting the status quo.

What is vs. what will be

Every company faces an inevitable tension between what it is and what it intends to become. Suppose you are an automaker and you truly believe that, by 2010, the biggest growth in the auto industry will come from electronic cars. Do you siphon off a larger share of money and talent and devote it to developing new transportation systems right now? What will you do to generate the financial windfall from today's automobiles or other revenue streams to fund the needed research and development for electronic cars?

Without question, the envisioned future shakes up short-term plans. But the opposite is also true. Today's choices and actions alter the course of the future. Imagine you are the CEO of a large retail chain that says, "Our foremost goal is to maximize operational efficiencies in order to stay cost competitive." Will your strategy of making major acquisitions to generate cost-cutting economies of scale produce a competitive advantage five years down the road? What if senior management's attention becomes so absorbed in milking cost savings out of today's acquisitions that they lose touch with shoppers' changing needs? Five years ahead, you may reach the point where there is no more fat to cut in expenses, and you are stocking products that are unappealing to your customers.

We no longer can afford the luxury of focusing all of our attention on the present or on the future. The future and the present are integrally linked to one another. Attempting to simplify matters by focusing on one or the other is ineffective.

Balancing short and long-term priorities sets up continual competition for resources, time, and focus of attention. But when push comes to shove, what is the right priority? Trendsetters have no doubt—favor the long term. Why such firm conviction? Because favoring the long term is the only choice when your goal is to invent business opportunities no one else can imagine.

In chaotic times, every change presents an opportunity to exploit. Voting irregularities in a Presidential election create demand for innovative products from manufacturers in the voting machine industry, or more likely, an outside industry trendsetter. If, in seven years, Chinese became the dominant language for the Worldwide Web, what chaos would that produce and what opportunities would emerge out of it? The premise is simple—unpredictability is a threat to replicators but an enormous opportunity for trendsetters.

This is the essence of Big Idea #1: Trendsetters simultaneously look at today's best opportunities and tomorrow's best bets and, when there's no clear winner, they favor the latter. This shift of priorities is the core of what it means to invent the future.

What inventing the future is NOT

Developing the capacity to invent the future requires a deeper understanding of the notion of "inventing." Let's first look at the four principle misconceptions replicators have about inventing the future.

It is not replication

Replicators try to perpetuate favorable market conditions for as long as possible. Overhauling a winning formula is out of the question. Tweaking it is an acceptable rate of change.

The apparent blindness to the danger of over-relying on a winning formula is captured in the words of Deng Xiaping: "When you are riding a dead horse, for heaven's sake—Dismount!"

Why do so many of us persist in trying to resuscitate a dying horse when we could hop on a fresh mount? Because we fail to notice the warning signs of decline that lie camouflaged among standard measures of business performance. Studying present-day financials alone will not help you separate yesterday's peak performers—companies whose best days are in the past—from those trendsetting companies poised for an explosive growth.

If the numbers don't provide an answer, how do we predict when replicating the formula for past success will no longer work? After studying numerous companies over the past 15 years, I have uncovered 10 telltale signs:

1. The competition has copied the company's cash cow products, and customers can't differentiate between them.

2. Achieving results comparable to those produced earlier, even just a few *months* earlier, requires significantly greater effort.

3. Management is obsessed with getting employees to implement the current strategy more effectively.

4. Employees argue more about who deserves credit for specific accomplishments than what's best for the company as a whole.

5. Strategizing for the future happens sporadically because everyone is dealing with unexpected opportunities or putting out fires.

6. Senior managers are under the gun to drive today's results through the roof, so developing the next cadre of leaders takes a backseat.

7. Top talent is jumping ship to more innovative competitors.

8. Employees are putting in longer hours and finding it more difficult to satisfactorily balance work and home life.

9. Profit margins are declining because customers are finding comparable products and services at a better price.

10. The cost of acquiring new customers and increasing market share is rising.

As these 10 indicators become more evident in your business, your winning formula will become less effective. To attain or regain competitive advantage, you must analyze the effectiveness of even the most sacred of your winning formulas. Replicating the past is like trying to ride a dead horse. It won't take you anywhere.

It is not improving reaction time

Another common misconception is to regard inventing the future as a task reserved for those rare visionaries who have uncanny ways of intuiting the next trend. Replicators assume that those who lack such visionary fore-sight should simply wait for the future to take shape, then react faster than anyone else.

There is one problem with this approach to handling the future: It is grounded in self-deception. We don't have the luxury of waiting for the future to unfold before staking out a strategic direction, because today's choices shape the future we will be reacting to. Today's choices about where to invest time and resources create the organizational foundation (talents, skills, competencies, assets, strategic alliances) for encountering future circumstances.

While our choices can only be exercised in the present, their impact simultaneously shapes the future. When choices take on a pattern, the impact is more pronounced and visible. Boiled down to a simple notion: *When you choose a habit, you also choose the future that comes with it.*

When we consistently max out our credit cards or invest astutely, we are determining the financial resources that will impact choices decades later in retirement.

When we choose lifestyle habits—remaining sedentary or engaging in regular exercise—we are determining our physical vitality today as well as in the future, and may even be influencing when we will die.

When we choose certain time management practices—being consumed with the rat race or spending a generous amount of our time fully present with loved ones—we are determining the quality of love and respect among our family members for years to come.

Similarly, when senior management routinely uses the previous year's winning formula as the basis for the current year's strategy, that decision will intensify the competitive battles of the future.

But when leaders rethink business plans to anticipate customers' latent needs, they are on the path to produce a strategic advantage that will defy competitors' attempts to copy them.

Businesses can no longer afford to wait for the future to emerge and then hope to replicate it faster and better. Every day they put off inno-vatively preparing for the future brings them another day closer to imple-menting antiquated plans.

It is not prediction

Predicting where an industry is headed is a preoccupying question at gatherings of supply channel members. Trade associations pay enormous sums to industry analysts and futurists to figure out how their industry will look in the future—5, 10, even 25 years from now.

But replicators place erroneous faith in forecasting. As futurist Richard Slaughter explains in his book *The Foresight Principle,* forecasts are based on if-then reasoning. They require careful analysis of past knowledge. They then assume that initial conditions will hold and current trends continue in order to predict a particular outcome with a certain level of confidence. For this reason, forecasts can be used as adjuncts to decision making, but should not be held as authoritative insights into the future. Slaughter contends that predicting any "single" future is actually impossible, because it fails to account for the active role of humans as agents of change.

Inventing the future requires an adjustment in how we process marketplace information. The core issue involves knowing when to forecast and when to favor foresight. Forecasting plays a more significant role in short-term planning, where there is a greater need and likelihood for accuracy in predication. Accurate predictions are essential for short-term resource allocation.

As the planning time frame lengthens and the focus is placed on innovation, crystal balls need to be put aside. A different kind of thinking—strategic foresight—is called for.

Strategic foresight involves imagining a desired future that you can make happen given changes that have already or might eventually occur. Trendsetters are proactive change agents who have a stake in bringing about a future that establishes them in a superior strategic position. Accordingly, strategic foresight requires more speculative, imaginative, and opportunistic thinking.

In the competitive game of strategic foresight, there is no single dominant future for any industry. There can be dozens of possible futures, limited only by what industry members can imagine. In developing bold strategy, imagination is more valuable than prediction.

It is not abandoning the past

The replicator's greatest fear of innovation is rooted in a misconception—that inventing the future requires jettisoning the past. There are some well-known examples that will help us put this worry to rest.

IBM isn't abandoning mainframes, even while its foreseeable future is in e-business.

Schwab didn't get rid of brokers, even though around half of its business is e-trading.

Disney retained its flagship theme park business, even when it expanded into broader entertainment venues like sports media (ESPN), athletic teams (California Angels, Anaheim Ducks), video entertainment, and management development (Disney Institute).

International Management Group continued to represent athletes while it expanded to sponsoring and managing sporting events.

Rather than *abandoning* the past, the central challenge of inventing the future is in *leveraging* the past. The most profitable innovations capitalize on relationships, core competencies, assets, customer knowledge, brand equity, infrastructure, strategic alliances, and best practices. The trick is to simultaneously abandon and exploit the past.

Prepare for the cat burglar

Now that the most common misconceptions about inventing the future have been corrected, the next step is to put Big Idea #1 into action. Trendsetters use three primary methods to insure their combination of long-range strategic priorities and short-term plans will reflect the proper amount of innovation: dual-focus leadership, strategic foresight, and imaginative future planning.

Dual focus leadership

In times of discontinuous change, one of the toughest leadership issues is determining where an organization's attention, energy, and resources are focused. If you concentrate solely on executing today's plans, you never see what lies around the curve until you're hit by tomorrow's market conditions. At the same time, if you look too far ahead into the future and lose touch with today's agenda, your short-term plans will lack crisp execution and steady accuracy in the midst of what seems like daily changes in market conditions.

As GE's CEO Jack Welch describes the dilemma, "You can't grow long-term if you can't eat short-term. Anybody can manage long. Balancing those two things is what management is." (*Business Week,*"Jack: A Close-up Look at How America's #1 Manager Runs GE," 6/8/98. P/ 92).

Escape from this quandary requires practicing a brand of setting priorities, better named, "dual focus leadership." In stable times, business people could routinely write out to-do lists containing actions that built linearly on the prior year's winning formula. But today's time allocation choices require a dual focus on weighing short and long-term implications. Dual focus leadership is the capacity to operate with integrated mind share of the past, present, and future tense in making more complex decisions. This integration of tenses facilitates learning from the past and doing (in the present) what it takes to usher in the desired future. Let's examine how the dimensions of tense—past, present, and future—get treated in an integrated fashion in the thinking process of a trendsetter.

The most profound access to power through dual focus leadership comes in recognizing that the future is not merely the outgrowth of a progression of past events. Rather, the past is seen as an organization's current foundation that must be adjusted, destroyed, or transformed to promote the envisioned future. While the past offers useful information, it does not become the template of successful precedents that must be carried forward to insure a successful future. Consequently, trendsetters treat the future as a vast opening of possibilities and choices, limited only by imagination. The future only exists as an imagined set of circumstances. In conceiving an original strategy, there is always a huge gap between what you're capable of doing in the present and what you need to be equipped to do in the future. The gap includes needed knowledge, core competencies, relationships, or the right organizational conditions (culture and structure) essential for implementing the long-term strategy. Closing the gap means allocating less time to continuous improvement activities that maintain past routines, while devoting more time and resources to projects that drive the future strategic position, such as: developing core competencies, product innovation R&D, reinventing roles, studying new minimally contested markets, pilot testing new products, and rethinking strategy. Gradually, priorities begin to shift to increasingly reflect work that supports the foundation for realizing the desired future.

Once priorities are fine tuned, it becomes apparent that the only tense where choices and actions can be exercised is in the present. The past exists in memory and the future exists in imagination—choice only exists in the present moment. For trendsetters, the present serves as the source of emotional fortitude to sustain vision-driven choices and actions in the face of newness and uncertainty, and even unwanted short term outcomes. Since the imagined future exists in the mind's eye, moment-by-moment decisions either advance or thwart the conversion of vision into reality.

A new relationship to time, planning, and readiness for change is required of trendsetters who are blazing a strategic trail for the first time and have no trail markers to follow in other's footsteps. As Watts Wacker, Jim Taylor, and Howard Means suggest in *The Visionary Handbook*, reinventing your relationship with time is essential, but doesn't come easy.

"By its very nature, the future destabilizes the present. By its very nature, the present resists the future. To survive, you need duality, but people and companies by their very nature tend to resist living in two different tenses." (Watts Wacker, Jim Taylor, Howard Means, *The Visionary's Handbook,* New York: HarperBusiness, 2000, p.77).

Dual focus leadership is not a natural way of thinking. Our thinking preferences gravitate to being oriented to either the past or the future. Plenty of leaders seek the comfort of building a business by leveraging past precedents. Many shortsighted entrepreneurs fall in love with imagining scenarios for the future, but find it unnatural to think about instilling the solid systems and structures that produce efficient operations.

It is easy to say "Maintain a dual focus" or "When push comes to shove, favor the decision that best serves the long-term future." It is quite another matter to lead by example.

When a manager tells me, "I can't study future trends. I've got a business to run," I take the remark as giving permission for the cat burglars to pillage. Plenty of managers, obsessed with hitting today's numbers, never look up to see what unexpected events might be looming around the corner. They just keep their heads down and hope they won't get blindsided. In contrast, many visionary entrepreneurs fall in love with imagined scenarios of the future, without constructing the systems for crisp execution and steady adjustments that insure proper cash flow.

My clients feel overwhelmed that they have the equivalent of two jobs—a day job where they work on present concerns, plus an after-hours job where they prepare for the future, such as learning new technology or preparing to enter global markets. Many feel they are in a no-win situation. The more effort they pour into preparing for the future, the less time they have to invest in the present, jeopardizing today's results. Given a choice, most people would opt to just do their day job and let the after-hours job slip. Unfortunately, this choice cripples any possibility for building a foundation for the future.

The demand for holding a dual focus can seem maddening, but only if we fail to appreciate how accurately it reflects our ever-changing business environment. Every decision must be based on how it will help you succeed today, *and* more important, how it will help you deliver on tomorrow's vision. Once the rationale for maintaining a dual focus makes sense, there is no point in fighting reality, so stress vanishes. Normalizing the healthy tension between present and future can be liberating. Freed from the confines of today's prerequisites, the pursuit of tomorrow's compelling vision can be exhilarating.

In executing an original strategy, the trendsetter recognizes the gap between what they are capable of doing in the present and what they need to be equipped to do in the future. Closing the gap means allocating less time to continuous improvement and reacting to crises. In turn, this shift of priorities frees up more time to develop core competencies, promote R&D, reinvent roles, study minimally contested markets, track future trends, and test and launch new products. Gradually, more time is spent in activities that support the desired future than in refining what has worked in the past.

Here is a list of dual-focus adjustments you can make in the following commonplace business activities:

Decision-making. Establish a decision-making process where team members always employ criteria that reflect both short- and long-term implications.

Job descriptions. Scrutinize job descriptions for relevance to today's and tomorrow's customers, both internal and external. Discuss how roles can be reinvented to better serve customers' future needs, then design positions accordingly.

Strategic planning. Establish the ground rule that strategic deliberations always include a dual focus. When targeting markets, consider those that are well established and those that are emerging. In analyzing competition, look at current competitors as well as companies that might eventually compete. When discussing distribution, contemplate current methods as well as novel channels for getting products to market.

Top-to-top customer meetings. Rethink the strategic value gained from meetings between the top executives of supplier firms and their commercial customers. Share future trends information that impacts your joint future; inquire into provocative strategic questions for which there are no easy answers; focus on co-creating an ideal relationship to deliver to your shared interests. For example, Johnsonville Sausage asks key retail accounts, "How would you define great performance from us as a manufacturer in this category?" The resulting definition of great performance then leads to mapping out the teamwork requirements for both parties to deliver on a shared vision of greatness.

Performance reviews. Besides appraising past performance strengths and limitations, the review is an excellent opportunity to talk about career aspirations. Conversations might include inventing roles that don't currently exist, but which are necessary to serve the emerging needs of external or internal customers.

Trade show debriefing sessions. When discussing what you learn from talking to customers, observing competitors booths, and attending educational seminars, go beyond planning for immediate sales opportunities. Broaden the discussion to include long-term implications for key account strategies, as well as new product or service ideas.

This list demonstrates only a few opportunities for dual-focus leadership in business matters. I recommend preparing your own list. Begin with your job description and primary responsibilities, the teams you're on; and, finally, the broader organizational matters that affect you indirectly. Keep considering how your customary work activities and company operations can be modified to encompass dual-focus planning.

Strategic foresight, not forecasting

While often used interchangeably, business forecasting and strategic foresight call for different types of thinking and produce different outcomes. Forecasting relies on logical reasoning and quantitative analysis to accurately predict the near future. Strategic foresight uses trend information and knowledge of ongoing changes to stir the imaginative thinking necessary to detect the novel opportunities likely to emerge in years ahead.

Trendsetters employ strategic foresight to discover intensifying latent needs and then conceive relevant products, services, and business models. A simplified way of portraying strategic foresight is by distinguishing three categories of information: industry trends, contextual trends, and current changes.

Industry trends include predications and future scenarios of industry leaders, industry experts, and trade association studies.

Contextual trends include legal, demographic, economic, agricultural, political, technological, environmental, and global trends, which offer predications about events that might materialize 10, 20, or 30 years from now. Futurists, think tanks, and government-sponsored studies are sources of these types of trends information.

The final category, changes already happening, includes events happening right before our eyes in movies, fashion, art, sports, religion, politics, books, and travel. This category includes changes anyone could observe at work, in their neighborhood, among family members, even by reading the *USA Today* Life section.

While all three categories of information are valuable, certain ones lend themselves to formulating truly original strategic foresight. Industry trends offer the least chance of separation from the competition. These trends are well known by all the major industry players, so there is nothing proprietary about them. Contextual trends offer an edge to companies who track information beyond the narrow confines of their industries. The broader sweep of trend information offers a better chance for developing original strategic foresight than competitors who only know industry trends. Both the industry and contextual trends are plausible assumptions about how the future might turn out, but they are not highly reliable.

Very often, the richest of the three categories is changes already happening. We don't know whether these changes will become enduring and encompassing trends, but they are real-life situations that a trendsetting organization can interact with in co-creating new products or services.

The founding of Starbucks is an impressive demonstration of strategic foresight that helped create the specialty beverage industry. Here are a few emerging trends Starbucks could have been aware of at the time of it's founding in the mid-1980s:

- Consumers were hassled and stressed out.
- Consumers were time-poor.
- Consumers placed high value on convenience.
- Consumers were aging.
- Consumers lacked a place to hang out between home and work.
- Consumers were working in home offices and telecommuting, and lacked much human interaction.
- Consumers were becoming more flavor-oriented.

- Consumers were rejecting imitations.
- Consumers were cost conscious and wanted the right value at an affordable price, especially when it came to coffee.
- Health conscious Baby Boomers were moving away from caffeine.

Howard Schultz, founder and CEO, got his original vision while attending a trade show in Italy where he was fascinated by the integral part coffeehouses play in the social life of Italian cities. He recognized that Americans needed a place outside of work and home, where they could feel safe, relax from the day's hectic pace, and where the environment was conducive to conversation, reading, or using a computer. In addition, he realized more and more consumers were working out of home offices and needed a relaxed place to meet with prospects and clients. From these insights, Schultz and company practically created an institution. Now exotic coffee drinks custom prepared in an attractive surrounding provide an affordable luxury for almost everyone.

The imagination of Starbucks leadership transformed a functional commodity product by infusing it with a dose of emotion. The power of this emotional connection results in an unwavering brand loyalty such that Starbucks now sells chocolates, jazz CDs, books from Oprah Winfrey's book club, water purifiers, even sandwiches and side salads.

Starbucks didn't figure out the dominant future where the coffee industry was headed—they invented it.

As Shultz foresaw, "If it captivates your imagination, it will captivate others." Starbucks founders leveraged their collective imagination to create a value offering based on a synthesis of consumer changes that were already apparent.

Which other companies had the same trend information about consumers? Nescafe, Maxwell House, and Folgers. These coffee powerhouses confined their product distribution to supermarkets and restaurants. They had the same data as upstart Starbucks, just not the same imagination.

Starbucks' success proves that signs of emerging trends are everywhere, for anyone to observe. But how do you learn to see them? By getting in the habit of practicing techniques that sharpen your imagination and develop your strategic foresight. Here are some suggested exercises:

Assemble a group of colleagues to track the three categories of trend information. During normal reading, TV watching, or conversations, the team's members should be alert to clipping or writing down trend information.

Each month, have the team prioritize the collection of trends that suggest growth opportunities for your business. Prioritize about a dozen opportunity-laden trends, looking for patterns in trends that seem to amplify the same customer needs.

Finally, the team should inquire into this set of questions: If x, y, and z became full-bore trends, which customer needs would intensify? If those customer needs intensified, which product or service offerings would become appealing?

Imaginative future planning

Cat burglars are threatening Fed Ex's long-standing advantage in service reliability. "What does Federal Express do now, in a world that may not absolutely, positively need it overnight?" asks Douglas Blackmon in a front-page article in *The Wall Street Journal.*

E-mail delivers documents instantly. UPS has a greater share of the booming consumer e-commerce deliveries. But even more foreboding, business customers are deploying new supply channel management systems that make the flow of materials more predictable. All these cat burglars are reducing demand for overnight service. If you were sitting in CEO Fred Smith's chair, what would you do?

True to its strategy, Fed Ex has repositioned itself as an inventory elimination business with select corporate accounts. Through a program called Emerge, Fed Ex aligns dozens of global shipments to a common just-in-time arrival point, virtually eliminating its customers' need to store inventory.

If your business is not currently facing a strategic crossroads like the one confronting Fred Smith, your high-stakes dilemma is coming soon.

Inventing the future is not optional; it is a survival imperative and it bears with it an uncomfortable truth: The more the envisioned future departs from current reality, the greater the risk of being ill-equipped to take the steps necessary to make it happen.

The growing gap between vision and reality calls for a shift in strategic planning methods, from a customary approach called "incrementalism," to the trendsetter's forte in "imaginative future planning." Incrementalism treats key business measures from the recent past as indicators of the organization's performance. This linear approach to strategic planning involves examining the key results of recent years (sales, costs, profitability) and adjusting them up or down a few percentage points for the next planning period. The vision of the future is an extrapolation of past results. Incrementalism conveys a preserve-the-status-quo bias anchored in a rigid historical view of customers, competitors, products, and services. The Fatal Assumption reigns. The future becomes hostage to past history.

Imaginative future planning radically departs from incrementalism and emphasizes a brand of thinking that is speculative, visionary, and expansive—one that challenges familiar patterns. It requires rethinking the following seven core elements that comprise a strategic position, typically targeted three to five years into the future:

What business are you in? A business can be defined in three ways—by its products and services, benefits to customers, and core competencies. This definition specifies the range of company products and services. It makes an enormous difference, for example, whether McDonald's categorizes itself as being in the hamburger or youth entertainment business; whether Nike is in the recreational footwear or athletic performance and fashion business; whether Harley-Davidson is in the motorcycle or lifestyle makeover business.

Who will be your future customers? Consider established markets and emerging markets. Be on the lookout for new ways of configuring markets, also referred to as "white space." At the time of their founding, industries like wellness, extreme sports, home improvement, and specialty beverages were considered white space.

Who will be your future competitors? Besides traditional competitors, this includes entire industries that might one day constitute competition. For instance, Microsoft and First Data Corporation produce on-line bill-paying software, which allows consumers to pay bills with the stroke of a computer key—no need to write checks provided by a local bank. Monster.com advertises jobs on-line nationwide, threatening one of the newspaper industry's main revenue sources.

What will be your future products and services? Go beyond product line extensions to invent products and services that introduce new value to targeted markets. Which of your current customer segments are defining value differently? For example, has the Internet caused them to define convenience of service by a new standard?

How will you go to market? The we've-always-done-it-this-way approach to sales and distribution should be treated as ripe for transformation. Stockbrokers did virtually all their business by phone, until Charles Schwab and E-Trade introduced on-line trading. Insurance policies, formerly sold exclusively by agents calling on prospects, are now available on-line. Manufacturers like Nike are jostling the supply channel by building their own retail stores and providing on-line ordering.

What core competencies will set you apart? In his book *Competing for the Future,* leading strategist Gary Hamel defined a core competency as, "a bundle of skills and technologies that enables a company to provide a particular benefit to customers." For example, Cisco's competence in managing strategic partnerships offers a steady supply of leading-edge technology solutions to key accounts. Starbucks' brand management gives customers a reliable quality assurance behind its products. Nike's product design satisfies the performance requirements of athletes and provides fashion for style-conscious consumers. Subway International's competence in franchise operations insures convenient access to products and consistent quality across the chain of stores.

What will be your primary competitive advantage? The strategic considerations of the first six elements ultimately comprise the source of a trendsetter's competitive advantage—how they deliver compelling and original value to their customers.

Rather than assuming current industry conditions will remain unchanged, imaginative future planning anticipates potential cat burglars and capitalizes on their destabilizing impact on the marketplace. The envisioned strategic position—all seven elements—represents an enormous stretch from current reality and cannot be achieved in the short term.

Plotting backward from the ultimate long-term strategic position, trendsetters determine a sequence of yearly foundational milestones, which describe the gradual changes in knowledge, technology, skills, culture, organizational structure, and network of strategic alliances that comprise the journey to the intended strategic position.

In a five-year plan, for example, imaginative future planning looks at the desired strategic position in five years and breaks it down to a sequence of milestones that build on each other. It asks the questions: To reach our intended strategic position five years from now, where do we need to be in four years? Three years? Two? One?

Ultimately, this sequence of foundational milestones aligns today's priorities and actions with tomorrow's envisioned strategic position.

Figure 2.1 on page 42 is an imaginative future planning tool used by my clients to insure that they systematically examine the various elements of a strategic position over a 10-year period. Here's how to use it:

By comparing your company's position five years ago to where it is today, you can diagram the historical progression of your strategy. Fill in the seven elements of a strategic position for both the "5 years ago" column and the "today" column. What does the comparison reveal? Is the strategy basically incrementalism, with no substantial change in strategic position over five years? Or do glaring changes in several of the seven elements indicate a commitment to carving out a strategically advantageous position?

The goal of strategic innovation is to reach different answers for some, if not all, of the elements for the column labeled "3-5 years from now." Once the new elements are decided, write them on the chart, and compare them to the "today" column to notice the proposed degree of change. This comparison prevents settling for play-it-safe incrementalism.

Figure 2.1. Summary of Elements of a Strategic Position

Elements	5 Years Ago	Today	5 Years From Now
Nature of the Business *(What business are you in?)*			
Future Customers *(Who will be your customers in the future?)*			
Future Competitors *(Who will be your future competition?)*			
Products and Services *(What will be your future products and services?)*			
Sales and Distribution Methods *(How will you go to market?)*			
Core Competencies *(What skill sets and technologies will set you apart?)*			
Source of Competitive Advantage *(What will be your primary competitive advantage?)*			

Scared, thrilled and free

Big Idea #1 reveals the trendsetter's fundamental choice in bold relief—invent a future or accept whatever results future circumstances permit. Getting in touch with your full capacity for entrepreneurial freedom can be both scary and thrilling. Depending on how you interpret the uncertain future, its emergence either threatens your past success or liberates you from the restraints of historic underpinnings.

We are witnessing the best time in business history for working backward from our imagined future to unfold a unique strategy.

Never before has there been such rich potential for targeting minimally contested market space and even inventing entirely new industries.

Never before have market boundaries been so permeable, permitting entry to newcomers with imagination and ideas.

Never before have the industry rule dictators been so consistently divested of market share by revolutionaries inventing the new rules.

It is time to reexamine established strategies and capitalize on the freedom of these uncertain times.

Chapter

3

The Jerry Garcia Principle

Chapter

3 The Jerry Garcia Principle

"You do not merely want to be considered the best of the best. You want to be considered the only one that does what you do."

—Jerry Garcia of the Grateful Dead

The notion of "differentiate or die" isn't extreme enough to describe the innovation required in today's competitive environment. A definition of the new standard came from an organization that achieved more than customer loyalty. Jerry Garcia and the Grateful Dead created a cult that commanded the allegiance of fans for 30 years. Credit goes to Jerry Garcia for coining the essence of Big Idea #2:

> **Big Idea #2: Be the only one that does what you do.**

Keeping up with the traditional best standards of your industry or profession isn't good enough. Sustainable advantage is reserved for those who offer one-of-a-kind value to their preferred market niche.

To paraphrase Justice Potter's famous remarks about pornography, we know an original company when see one. There is only one Nordstrom, one Crate and Barrel, one Toys 'R' Us, one Disney, one Victoria's Secret, one McDonald's, one Microsoft and one Ritz-Carlton. When you look at celebrated individuals, there

How do you become known as "the only one to do what you do"?

is only one Martha Stewart, one Picasso, one Ralph Nader, and one Steven Spielberg.

When you are the only one to do exactly what you do in your industry, customers that want your value offering have no other choice but to come to you. Starbucks' drinkers won't accept Maxwell House. Nike customers won't trade in their Air Jordans for a shoe from Reebok. Barry Manilow fans aren't interested in tickets for a Madonna concert. Competing with a trendsetter is like following Elvis or the Beatles on The Ed Sullivan Show.

While there are many trendsetter wannabes, the quest for unquestionable originality is mastered by few. Witness the familiar industry scenario where everyone else plays catch-up to one recognizable trendsetter. Notice business ventures that have their flash of brilliance, only to find that the competition copies or even exceeds their innovation. So what is the illusive magic in trendsetter strategies that enables them to sustain their astounding distinctiveness for years, even decades?

Four prototypes for strategy development

Whether a business is primed for replication or innovation is reflected in the thinking of its strategists. Eavesdrop on a meeting in the replicator camp and you might hear statements like: "We need to protect ourselves from making costly mistakes," or "We'll react fast once change in the industry solidifies." Eavesdrop on a trendsetter's conversation and you might hear, "We'd better cannibalize our business before someone else does," or "Let's watch where the industry is heading, then move in the opposite direction."

The root assumptions held by senior management about competing, risk tolerance, and creativity determine how strategies unfold. Without a change in the root assumptions, don't expect a humdrum strategy to be transformed into trendsetting originality at the upcoming senior management retreat. Nevertheless, few companies bother to lay bare the core assumptions that underpin their business approaches. Now is the time to clarify the root assumptions that reside in your company by examining the four basic prototypes for strategy development. Here are two replicator strategies that build on the past—their own history and their competition's.

Conformists

Change disturbs business routines, so conformists respond judiciously when customers make requests that don't fit their existing product and service offerings. With moderate accounts or small market segments, they reply, "Sorry we don't do that," and treat the unusual appeal like an intrusion rather than an opportunity. For major accounts, they may reluctantly acquiesce.

Here is an abbreviated scouting report on conformists:

- *Trend sensitivity:* Conformists focus most of their attention on maintaining close connections with individual accounts or targeted customer segments. They know what is happening at a micro level, but fail to consider the big picture, or develop a futuristic view of the market. Macro opportunities elude them.

- *Risk tolerance:* Conformists don't read the handwriting on the wall until their backs are against it. They are unwilling to risk change unless they are left with no other options.

- *Customer perception:* Conformists adequately serve well-known needs in the marketplace. They attract customers who are treading water, not progressive businesses that are swimming upstream to the future. They are definitely not the supplier of choice for early adopters of innovation.

- *Strengths:* Conformists do a good job of deriving maximum earnings from their cash cows. They expend minimal resources on R&D, market research, and educating customers about new products and services. Successful conformists have enough customers who are satisfied with having their basic requirements met—at least for now.

- *Weaknesses:* Conformists' strengths are also their weaknesses. On the surface, their well-defined niche appears to guarantee steady profits. But underlying this seemingly enviable picture, the conformists' concentration on their best customers prevents their seeking out and capitalizing on new minimally contested markets. Even among their best customers, conformists pay attention only to well articulated needs, and remain oblivious to their customers' unexpressed issues. The result is lost opportunities for penetrating key business accounts or gaining an enlarged share of the consumer's wallet.

Copycats

No CEO would dream of telling shareholders or employees, "Our compelling vision is to one day become a world class 'me-too' company!" Such an admission hardly inspires peak performance.

Yet a large percentage of businesses actually communicate a disguised version of that message to their constituents. They mask their true intentions with words like, "We realize that no company can predict the future accurately and we don't want to waste money on risky ventures that go nowhere. Let the competition try out innovations and take the risks. If their innovation is a hit we'll play catch-up." Beneath the rhetoric lies the unvarnished truth: We choose to be followers. We choose not to have an original strategy.

The copycat strategy is a compromise. It doesn't address emerging customer needs until the competitors' moves clearly signal where the industry is headed. Armed with the safety of numbers, the copycat follows the pack.

Copycats are always playing catch up to their industry's trendsetters. Think of Burger King chasing McDonald's, Avis trying harder to catch Hertz, or McDonnell-Douglas following Boeing. Think of Fujitsu behind IBM's trail in mainframes, Reebok sprinting to keep pace with Nike, or Kmart in pursuit of Wal-Mart. Colgate settles for seeing itself as "second to Procter" and on a quest to be "another P&G."

Here's how to spot a copycat company:

- *Trend sensitivity:* Copycats are vigilant observers of their competitors' innovations. They capitalize on trends only after the initial business opportunity has been developed.

- *Risk tolerance:* Copycats act only when a new innovation has proven profitable. They let their competition do the field-testing.

- *Customer perception:* Copycats are among the first targets of price reduction negotiations.

- *Strengths:* Copycats let their competitors absorb the costs of R&D and initial marketing of new products or services. Then they leverage the savings into a profitability and pricing advantage.

- *Weaknesses:* Copycats miss out on the advantages that come with being first to exploit a fresh opportunity: lucrative sales growth, improved market share, and higher margins. They have to compete largely on price or special promotions once the innovation's novelty wears off.

Copycat strategies face serious jeopardy when a competitor comes up with a hard-to-copy innovation or when the window of opportunity slams shut faster than anticipated. This threat to profitability soars when nontraditional competitors that are off the copycat's radar screen introduce innovations.

By contrast, here are two trendsetter strategies that invent new futures, but in different ways.

Best of the bests

While they are never first to market, best-of-the-best companies come on like gangbusters once the innovation is launched. Their goal is to unseat the originator in the minds of customers. Unlike copycats, best of the bests aren't satisfied with duplicating innovations. Their objective is to master innovations more effectively than the originator. When they are successful, the primary innovator's name is forgotten. The best-of-the-best company earns the brand equity.

In the auto and electronics industries, Japanese manufacturers are masters of this strategy. In high technology, most people don't realize that

Xerox invented the earliest prototype personal computer, the mouse, and point-and-click computing. We only remember the companies that did it best, like Apple.

In software, Microsoft's competitors are dumbfounded by the company's steady dominance. They are frustrated because Microsoft rarely conceives technological advances, yet winds up with the brand equity for the innovation. Renowned for hiring the best and brightest, the company depends on this brainpower to quickly overtake a competitor's budding innovation. If Microsoft's own talent can't figure it out fast enough, look for Bill Gates and company to partner with the first player to go to market or acquire the necessary competencies. And once the product is ready to ship, watch the massive Microsoft marketing machine stage a new product rollout that competitors can only envy.

The book on best-of-the best companies contains these primary points:

- *Trend sensitivity.* Best-of-the-bests know the key trends but don't synthesize the information to conceive business opportunities. They exploit trends by following the trail of the primary innovators with the intent of catapulting past them in market penetration and name recognition.
- *Risk tolerance.* Best-of-the-bests are confident in their ultimate ability to surpass the first-to-market player. They are willing to risk missing a strong share of early sales, and require evidence of a successful innovation before launching efforts to provide superior value.
- *Customer perception.* Best-of-the-bests can't be counted on to lead the way to the future, but will eventually be major players in bringing innovation to a defined market segment. Customers trust that best-of-the-best companies won't entice them to adopt some half-baked idea before it is user-ready.
- *Strengths.* Best-of-the-best companies have an outstanding ability to acquire or develop mastery of a competitor's innovation, and execute it with even better proficiency or profitability. They rely heavily on their talented employees to

out-think, out-hustle, and eventually leapfrog the original inventor.

- *Weaknesses.* In toe-to-toe competition, equally or more talented competitors may get so far ahead that there is no chance for the best-of-the-best company to build on their shoulders.

Catalysts for innovation

Innovation catalysts conceive of a trend long before it becomes front-page news, and generate momentum that accelerates the trend and magnifies its expression in the marketplace. For at least a brief window of time, innovation catalysts are certain of being the only one to do what they do. They use expansive language like "creating something from nothing," "pushing the envelope," and "inventing a future that wasn't ordinarily going to happen." Give us your revolutionaries, rule breakers, contrarians, paradigm pioneers, dreamers, thought leaders, and mavericks!

Innovation catalysts scorn industry conventions, and aggressively shrug off the yoke of conformity, preferring to imagine what might be possible. In most markets, customers are basically satisfied with the industry's current value offering, until an innovation catalyst introduces one that's obviously superior. Think of products like e-mail, cellular phones, ATM machines, cable, and CDs. Think of services like personal fitness trainers and website designers. Suddenly, the thinking in the marketplace goes from, "We don't need that," to "How did we ever get along without it?" Ultimately, innovation catalysts seek to accelerate the full emergence of a new market trend by actually creating customer needs.

While being first is no guarantee of being the long-term market leader, Ira Blumenthal in *Ready, Blame, Fire!* offered these examples of innovation catalysts who have endured in their first-to-market position: Blockbuster Video, Coca-Cola, Dixie Cup, Dr. Scholl's (foot aids), Gillette (safety razor), Proctor and Gamble (Ivory Soap), Lea & Perrins (Worcestershire Sauce), Murine (eye care products), and 3M (Scotch Tape). And I would add to that list Canon, Charles Schwab, CNN, Edward Jones,

Enron, Enterprise Rent-A-Car, ESPN, Gold's Gym, Home Depot, Nike, Nucor, 7-Eleven, Sharper Image, Southwest Airlines, Starbucks, and Ticket Master.

The following encapsulizes the innovation catalyst position:

- *Trend sensitivity.* Innovation catalysts don't merely understand trends, report trends, or forecast trends. They create them. They are masters at recognizing latent customer needs and introducing compelling innovations to the marketplace.

- *Risk tolerance.* Innovation catalysts' motto is: If it works, it's obsolete. They are willing to bite the bullet and lose money launching an innovation.

- *Customer perception.* Innovation catalysts are viewed as pace setters for the industry. When it comes to leading-edge products and services, customers have no other choice for doing business—period. Innovation catalysts have an uncanny ability to know what customers want before they ask, and their brand is associated with innovation, imagination, and cool products.

- *Strengths.* Innovation catalysts are number one in the minds of customers who depend on being aligned with pace setters to guide them to the future. Best-of-the-best companies take a back seat to an innovation catalyst's imagination, strategic foresight, and risk tolerance.

- *Weaknesses.* Innovation catalysts pay a substantial price for making mistakes in the bold game of being first. At the outset, strong agreement in the marketplace about the need for their products or services may be missing. Innovation catalysts require a lucrative trial-and-error budget for field-testing and multiple refinements, as well as for promotions to educate customers and whet their appetites for the innovation. To recoup these high upfront costs, innovation catalysts are often confined to being high-price providers (unless of course, their innovation produces cost efficiency and price reduction). Even worse, after all that effort, being first is no guarantee they will always be perceived as the best.

So where does this discussion of the four strategy prototypes leave you? Which prototype is most closely aligned to the assumptions that underpin the strategies of your business? Don't sit on the fence in responding to this question. Take an honest look and decide which one is dominant.

Sometimes a company doesn't fit neatly into just one of the four strategies. For example, the vice president of sales for an electronics distributor determined that his company was a trendsetter in its most lucrative markets, and a replicator in the more price-sensitive segments. Since some of his customers just wanted his product cheap and easy-to-acquire, they didn't need a trendsetting supplier.

In another example, the CEO of a holding company that included a diverse array of real estate development and recreational sports businesses realized that his managers would "be blown away at the prospect of changing the entire company into trendsetters." He concluded that his exclusive urban apartment properties were trendsetting ventures, while his other businesses simply compared well with competitors. He also appreciated that the confidence and competencies gained from being a trendsetter in one business could accelerate the gradual transformation of his replicator businesses.

How to Achieve a Sustainable Advantage

While strategists would like nothing better than certainty and permanence in executing their plans, the reality can be compared to the eroding interaction of natural forces on a beach. On the beach, lines in the sand are wiped out in minutes in the face of pounding surf and cascading ocean spray. Erosion of business advantages is also a natural way of life in the competitive marketplace. No matter where you draw the strategic line today, there is no guarantee of retaining your standing in the face of changing customer needs and evolving competitor strategies. History is filled with examples of one-time trendsetters who enjoyed their time at the head of the pack, but slipped back to being replicators.

One or two strategic misfires were all it took to ignite the fall of a high technology empire, as demonstrated in the case of Apple in the early

1990's. Business pundits have had a field day poking holes in Apple's post-Macintosh strategic blunders:

- **Slow to see the laptop market.** "Apple was late in getting into laptop computers, competing against well-entrenched laptop leaders as Toshiba, NEC, Tandy, Zenith Data, and Compaq." (*BusinessWeek,* March 18, 1991.)

- **Failure to succeed in the business market.** "Sporadic and ineffective efforts over a decade have left the Macintosh with just 5.8 percent of the business market, not enough to excite software writers. Now the Mac is behind in client/server programs, a must in corporate computing." (*BusinessWeek,* October 3, 1994.)

- **Insistence on proprietary technology.** "Despite vigorous in-company debate, Apple has historically refused to let other companies put its famous, easy-to-use Mac technology on their PCs. Rival Microsoft, however, created a Mac-like operating system called Windows, which has become a huge hit… The royalties from allowing PC makers to use Windows has helped make Microsoft a PC industry titan. Indeed Apple's refusal to license others ranks as one of the industry's greatest blunders." (James Kim, *USA Today,* November 7, 1994.)

Perhaps the ultimate comment on Apple's fall came from Bill Fernandez, Apple's first engineer, after being laid off in 1993. "When we started, we considered ourselves pirates, doing something revolutionary. There are no pirates today."

Given the inevitable impact of eroding factors, how do trendsetters maintain their advantage? For one thing, they don't put their energy into beating back competitive thrusts. Trendsetters devote their creative and intellectual energies toward an entirely different objective—avoiding competition whenever possible. Instead of fighting for the same customer, the same share of market, with the same value offering, they out-think competitors in creating a groundswell of customer demand for their one-of-a-kind value proposition.

As Walt Disney once said, "It's always fun to do the impossible because there's less competition."

Four major criteria typically exist in strategies that give trendsetters a sustainable advantage.

Develop original foresight about future markets

If your competition heard your view of the future of the marketplace, would they respond with a yawn of boredom or would their jaws drop at its originality?

An original viewpoint requires enlarging a management team's perspective about the future marketplace. Reading the same trade publications, attending the same industry conferences, and confining networking to industry colleagues are sure ways to perceive the future just like everybody else. Original strategic foresight requires the ability to creatively synthesize trends such as technology, demographics, legislation, economics, and lifestyles.

Trendsetters aren't content to adopt the prevailing consensus of how an industry's future will unfold. They are obsessed with conceiving a viewpoint for the future that dramatically departs from how an industry has historically defined its products and services or delivered them to the marketplace.

Holding an original viewpoint demands concentration on trends that are taking shape today or that will exert influence in three to ten years, and accounting for them when mapping long-term strategy. The question to ask is: Given the way the future might shake out, what will be the source of our distinctive competitive advantage in the years ahead?

Who is America's most innovative company? Would you believe Enron, a natural gas and electricity supplier? This firm was ranked number one out of more than 400 companies for six years in a row on *Fortune's* most admired companies survey. Anticipating the deregulation of the gas industry in the 1980s and electricity in the early 1990s, Enron deduced that pricing elasticity and the breakup of local energy monopolies would soon follow. In addition, they adapted the real-time model of the financial markets to the purchase of natural gas and electricity. As a result, commercial customers could develop energy portfolios based on their choice of pricing by figuring in long- or short-term considerations, or going with the market index.

Enron is pioneering a new business model in e-trading. Most Web sites connect buyers and sellers by letting companies post their products and then taking a small percentage of transactions. Enron acts as an intermediary in each trade, guaranteeing commodities purchased on its sites are delievered at the price and terms agreed upon. Profits come from the spread between what Enron pays for a commodity and what it sells for.

In 2000, Enron Broadband Services built a communications network over fiber located in its existing interstate gas pipeline network. The long-term plan is to trade telecom bandwidth space on its network and those built by other companies. Enron will be able to quickly find available bandwidth and generate contracts for much shorter terms than those now favored by telecom companies.

Enron is applying its e-trading model to paper, metals, coal, and even financial instruments that let snowmobile makers hedge against mild winters. Could the day come, in the future, when consumers will follow the price of Wheaties the way brokers trace the share price of General Mills?

Another company with an original vision for the transportation industry is Toyota. In response to congested city traffic, car noise, limited petroleum supplies, and air pollution, Toyota is developing an advanced commuter transportation system featuring electronic vehicles (EVs). The company is experimenting with two-seat personal transport EVs for business park operations on a shared membership system in Irvine, California.

Here's how the system works. Using a PC, each driver inputs three pieces of information: choice of car sharing station, destination, and time of use. The driver arrives at the station car depot that is conveniently reachable by mass transit, and places the Crayon card on a terminal for activation. Upon reaching the assigned car, the driver holds the card to the card reader to gain access to the vehicle, which eliminates the need for sharing keys. The electric charge is fully automated. All the driver has to do is insert the inductive charging paddle into the receptacle at the front of each vehicle.

The system control center pinpoints each car's location, and alerts drivers to stay in the designated driving area, monitors the battery charge status, and allocates cars with the appropriate charge to reach a given destination. The car also has an on-board navigation system that informs drivers about traffic congestion and suggests alternative routing. Usage charges are billed electronically when the card is returned to the terminal.

While the initial field-testing is being conducted in office parks, Toyota's vision is to expand the shared transportation concept to residents of local communities and rental car systems at resorts and tourist spots. By adopting an original viewpoint about the future of transportation, Toyota develops separate elements of technology in use today into an integrated system.

To develop an original viewpoint requires broadening the information you attract by studying information outside your industry, hiring people from other industries, engaging in executive education opportunities with leaders from other industries, even studying innovations or novel practices while you travel overseas.

Focus on creating minimally contested market space

Industries are typically differentiated on the basis of incremental improvement in cost, quality, or both. Accordingly, when markets become flat, strategic moves to boost sales growth become more complex. One increasingly frequent challenge occurs when the low-price leader position in the marketplace seems reserved for a few companies massive enough to achieve superior economies of scale. The other scenario is when product quality measures are at an all time high, and achieving noticeable differences seems impossible.

Trendsetters aren't interested in becoming market-share combatants battling for the same customers. While replicators search to improve price and quality, trendsetters are hard at work seeking out minimally contested market space. The following are examples of companies that created new markets or regenerated existing markets by introducing new value, rather than going head-to-head with their competitors.

- Southwest Airlines created a new market by catering to travelers who would gladly fly, rather than drive, if someone scheduled flights to their short-hop destinations at reasonable prices. Southwest, of course, did exactly that.
- Eastman Kodak's disposable cameras target children and vacationing adults who forget their cameras.
- Champion Enterprises sells low-cost, quick-to-build prefabricated houses for customers whose only other option is renting or buying an apartment.
- Options by Stafford, a JC Penney line, targets men who are baffled by what to wear for dress-down Fridays or business casual occasions, and who realize they can't wear golf course attire to a meeting in a city hotel.
- As more states legalize the gaming industry, Las Vegas is converting itself into a family vacation destination (MGM Grand Hotel), and even more recently to a location for elite hotels (Belaggio, Monte Carlo, Mandeley Bay), which provide first-class treatment at lower prices than comparable tourist meccas like New York, San Francisco, or Paris.

In each example, trendsetters conceived a new market that was invisible to their replicator counterparts, who were busy upgrading their value offering within conventionally defined market boundaries. Trendsetters stand for revolutionizing and expanding markets, the only limits being imposed by their own imagination and risk tolerance.

Reinvent the rules of competition

Any industry has three categories of players: incumbents, adaptors, and revolutionaries.

Incumbents build the industry and do everything in their power to insure that the rules of competition that defined their success remain intact.

Adapters politely accept and play by the established rules.

Revolutionaries, like the following three companies, rewrite the rules by introducing new business models.

- Dell Computers builds customized computers with a direct business model that nearly eliminates inventory costs through continuous replenishment of actual orders.
- Amazon.com sells books without a single retail outlet and with nearly 100 percent electronic transactions.
- Edward Jones outflanks mainstream brokerage houses by adapting Wal-Mart's strategy of planting offices, the majority single-broker, in small-town America.

Let's look at one emerging revolutionary rule breaker in greater depth. RCN, based in Princeton, New Jersey, envisions providing a one-stop, bundled service of local and long distance phone service, Internet access, and cable TV. CEO David McCourt's sense of reinventing an industry came across in his statement to shareholders, "Yesterday's networks simply do not have the capacity to respond to the demands of tomorrow. RCN is tomorrow, a company committed to evolving in a dynamic industry, even as our competitors court extinction."

McCourt sees the traditional telecommunications and cable incumbents entrenched in out-of-date technology that is very costly to revamp. Using fiber optic systems that allow for higher bandwidth capacity, RCN is attempting to offer hard-to-beat value by becoming a low-cost provider that offers superior technology. Once the technology is in place, service possibilities are endless. RCN is talking about adding services like a concierge morning wakeup and even home security.

By ignoring traditional industry boundaries and bundling diverse services, RCN is accelerating the dawn of the digital age. The exciting possibility is to become the primary linkage for "smart homes" which join communications, entertainment, energy, on-line retailing, and security, with the information needed to increase the efficiency of all these services.

Dr. Roger Blackwell in *From Mind to Market* describes the mind-boggling competitive advantage: "The company that coordinates all roads entering the consumers' homes will be the gatekeeper to their minds, their needs, and their pocketbooks."

Offer hard-to-copy value

The trendsetter's strategy may seem crystal clear to competitors, but history proves that copying them is not easy. The strategies emphasize four factors that are practically copy resistant: company culture, original conception of a business, core competencies, and design mindfulness.

Create a company culture that conveys unsurpassed performance. The best brands create not only distinctiveness, but also an emotional connection with the customer. This connection is based not so much on tangible products such as designer jeans, hotel rooms, or ice cream. It is built on intangibles—personality and unsurpassable service.

Imagine you are on the TV quiz show, *Jeopardy.* You select "Corporate Brands" for $100. The answer is: "A retailer willing to make unreasonable effort to exceed customer expectations." Instantly you hit the buzzer and ask: "What is Nordstrom?" The great majority of people playing along in the studio or at home would have said exactly the same thing.

You are on a roll. "Corporate Brands for $200." The second answer is "A hotelier renowned for elegant service." Hit the buzzer: "What is Ritz Carlton, Alex?" Correct again!

Company culture can play an enormous role in creating a distinctive brand identity. It is not uncommon to hear a CEO or manager say they aspire to become the Nordstrom of their industry. If it's not Nordstrom, just fill in Microsoft, Disney, or another highly admired company. While would-be emulators may replicate some of the observable elements of these trendsetters' success, it is probably impossible to copy the purpose, values, and norms that drive a company's choices and actions—in other words, the culture. If culture can't be copied, then the advantages it brings become sustainable.

Articulate an original conception of your business. A second powerful source of a brand's emotional connection is what business it perceives itself to be in. Harley Davidson isn't selling motorcycles. It supports the lifestyle of people who love the freedom of the open road. As COO Jeff Bleustein said, "When we talk about the company, we talk about the institution. We all think we're part of something bigger. We're stewards of a company for a much larger group of people to whom Harley Davidson means so much."

Mail order cataloguer Republic of Tea transformed tea from a poorly marketed commodity to a welcome, relaxing treat, a departure from the fast-paced, uptight world.

Check out the advertising for Timberland Company. It contains photos of their leather goods, but the copy is devoted to inspiring messages about the American Dream, heroism, and an individual's power to make a difference.

Nike's brand is associated with reverence for the human spirit expressed in athletic competition and the pursuit of excellence through physical training.

The Container Store originated the category of storage organization in 1978, and decades later, other retailers still haven't focused on the same inventory mix. As specialty retailers, they sell merchandise that doesn't sell itself, relying on salespeople to relate stories about the product. They take products only available for commercial use and convert it to practical consumer applications: egg baskets as carryalls, wire leaf burners as toy barrels, milk crates that pass as file containers or bedside tables in a college dorm. These original concepts of product use make The Container Store extremely difficult to copy, and their functional products reduce customers' stress.

When a company brings an original concept of the business into an industry dominated by companies with similar viewpoints, innovation is virtually assured. Traditionally, the airline industry is focused on maximizing operational efficiencies. Along comes Virgin Atlantic Airlines, influenced by its diverse industry portfolio (records, entertainment megastores, radio stations, consumer banks, and a passenger train service), and you end up with a very unique airline. Instead of a bias for cost containment and resulting service compromises, Virgin focuses on making the airline experience fun, valuable for the money, and filled with customer feel-good innovations.

CEO Richard Branson's unorothodox airline innovations include on-board video games, in-flight bars, masseuses and manicurists, beds and baths for business class, and jacks for recharging laptops. With boundless imagination, Branson conceives a children's section with nannies offering entertainment to kids, and even a dating section, where passengers can send messages to suggest a seat move to facilitate getting acquainted with someone they find attractive. Branson's vision is literally out of this world—Virgin Galactic Airways is already formed to someday take passengers into outer space.

The emotional connection with customers comes from the unique vantage point from which a company regards its business, not the tea, motorcycles, or shoes. Distinctive products and branding arise from viewing your business like no one else does.

Boost core competencies. Imagine how difficult it would be for a competitor starting from scratch to copy Sony's core competence in "miniaturization?" As a newcomer lacking the foundation of accumulated knowledge, skills, and technologies, it would take years to copy a pocket-sized Sony product.

Notice how other retailers are trying to cut costs to match Wal-Mart, without significantly closing the gap? Wal-Mart's state-of-the-art logistics integrates several technologies, making their systems extremely hard to copy.

McDonald's enduring success can be attributed to a collection of core competencies including real estate selection, fast and reliable systems of food preparation, food distribution networking, supplier relationships, franchising, global branding, and youth entertainment. To compete with McDonald's requires mastering a broad-range of core competencies.

Developing a core competence requires substantial investment of time and resources. The decision to master a core competence marks a point of departure from the rest of the competitive pack, being able to develop products and services that exceed all your competitor's skill sets and knowledge capacities.

Operate with design mindfulness. Design choices show up in every aspect of a business: from product displays, to colors and sizes of product, to the style of service and store formats.

Design mindfulness means operating with a distinctively appealing treatment in the way you conceive products, services, and systems of distribution. It is an expression of taste, aesthetic judgment, passion for the product, and care for the customer. Think about Gillette's Lady Sensor. Think about how the Coke bottle is shaped. Notice the stark look and feel of *Fast Company* magazine compared to the others on the newsstand. Its distinctive combination of paper, type, and color earned several "magazine design of the year" awards, winning against publications that had famous athletes and movie stars to decorate the pages.

Even customer service systems can be designed with original flair. Disney designs every detail of their guests' experience, such as providing warm up shows to "shorten" long waits at venues, and computerized systems to locate hard-to-find cars in an enormous parking lot. Mapping the precise distance between garbage disposal units determines whether a candy wrapper hits the ground or gets deposited in a trash receptacle.

While competitors do attempt to mimic design judgment, their efforts usually come off looking tired and uninspired. Like a wannabe oil painter trying to copy a Flemish master, the distinctive artistic flare resists duplication. Imitators fall short of matching up with the trendsetter's judgment and self-expression. They are not authentic.

The Jerry Garcia Principle in Action

"Be the only one to do what you do" is more than a great sound bite from an interview with Jerry Garcia. It is the core strategy behind his group's success and that of all one-of-a-kind companies. Let's explore in depth how, this strategy is reflected in two different industries: entertainment and continuing education.

Much more than rock music

By any business measure, the Grateful Dead was one of the most sophisticated and successful touring and merchandising ventures in the history of rock music. With fans spanning three generations, Grateful Dead Merchandising and the Grateful Dead band grossed in excess of $50 million in 1995, the year of Jerry Garcia's death and about 30 years after its founding. This demonstration of sustained customer appeal is remarkable in an industry where today's hit group almost inevitably becomes tomorrow's has-been.

"We weren't really in the music business," said Dennis McNally, the band's longtime publicist, "We were in the Grateful Dead business."

Here is the briefest summary of their business accomplishments:

- No. 1 grossing touring band in 1991 and 1993.
- A mailing list of 90,000 "Deadhead" fans
- A catalog of nearly 200 band-related items.
- *Relix*, a Grateful Dead magazine, boasted 220,000 readers.
- A line of successful "Dead" art and logos, which have appeared on products from Christmas cards to cyberDead computer and CD programs.
- "Cherry Garcia," a Ben & Jerry's Ice Cream flavor, spurred by fan appeal.
- Clothing accessories—imagine Deadhead executives shopping at Bloomingdale's and Macy's for J. Garcia neckties. (Garcia probably never wore a necktie in his life!)

The Dead's uniqueness is captured in the *San Francisco Chronicle* editorial entitled "American Beauty," which eulogized the passing of Jerry Garcia: "In an industry that thrives on hype, glitz, and greed, Garcia...and the band offered open and accessible celebration and entertainment to their countless Deadhead fans, who were treated as members of an extended family, not as suckers to be fleeced."

A national hotline for ticket sales allowed loyal fans to bypass ticket service charges, allowing them to buy tickets before the general public for $2–$3 off the gate price. Unlike most rock concerts, where tape recorders are checked at the door, fans could bring their recorders and sit in a special taping section to pick up the best sound quality.

Dead concerts were typically multi-day gatherings where local artisans and merchants sold their merchandise in proximity to the concert venue without paying exorbitant fees. This "impromptu marketplace" appealed to fans that enjoyed mingling for days, not merely for the few hours of the actual concert. The band took a stand for social action, including sharing concert funds with Greenpeace to counter the destruction of tropical rain forests.

Perhaps the most telling point of originality is the music, which doesn't fit neatly into any category, but represents a unique fusion of styles. Being the only ones to do what they did paid off in the wallet and in the soul, with "integrity" to their music and fans being the most constant adjective running through the remarks of Deadheads and music industry commentators.

Let's now move from rock n' roll to another business that had the same strategic intent to achieve "no-other-choice" distinctiveness.

A dental conference as a labor of love

As a speaker who has given presentations at more than 1,000 corporate and trade association events, it takes a lot to impress me. But I was blown away by the carefully conceived design choices at the January 2001 Annual Symposium of the Seattle Study Club, a continuing dental education network.

My initial sense of being involved in an extraordinary experience began when my pre-conference brochure arrived in a cylinder filled with drafting sheets that looked like architect's blueprints. The materials symbolized the conference theme, which likened crafting a dental practice to architects at a drafting board.

On site, the surprises continued. During the mid-morning break, a harp player soothed the throng in the exhibit booth area. A team of six balloon-tossing clowns pranced through the aisles, entertaining the 300 dentists and their spouses assembling in the ballroom.

The four-day conference contained sessions on clinical treatment and dental practice management, punctuated by diverse performers. One afternoon agenda juxtaposed a standup comedian followed by a Holocaust survivor. How would any meeting planner consider putting an audience through such a dramatic emotional shift?

Not printed on the program, but inserted between two speakers, was a surprise appearance of the Seattle Children's Choir singing heartrending songs about human perseverance.

I left the conference convinced I had witnessed a dental conference no competitor could dream of copying.

Seattle Study Club (SSC) is the vision of its founder, Dr. Michael Cohen. With 152 chapters throughout the United States and Canada, the organization's mission is to elevate the quality of dentistry in a community, build strong relationships among referring dentists, and take members' practices to a higher level of success.

Suzanne Cohen, Michael's wife and co-designer, is very clear on their over-riding principle of design: "While we know who our ideal customer is, Michael and I are more driven to express what's inside of us than to deliver a brand message based on what the market wants to hear. Michael loves music, architecture, and orchestrating a production." Rather than offering a dry series of professional education courses, SSC uses their emphasis on self-expression to differentiate their conferences from all others in the industry.

"We intersperse off-the-wall entertainment throughout the program because it quickens the mind and the senses, says Suzanne. "Since the participants don't know what to expect, the whole experience keeps their attention and is often a source of unusual learning."

Clearly the SSC style of program is not for every dentist. But the design choices communicate a compelling value to their enthusiastic members. As Suzanne notes, "Everything we do is a labor of love. That's a very powerful and inspiring business model for most people."

Whether you are a rock band or a dental education network, the point is always the same: When you are the only one to do what you do, it's a lot more fun, and, for your dedicated devotees, there is no other choice.

What if Jack Welch were coaching you?

My brother, Marty, worked for General Electric Plastics and Silicones for 20 years and used to participate in top management meetings with CEO Jack Welch. Marty was particularly impressed with Welch's performance monitoring practices. When Welch conducted performance reviews, Marty explained, he expected GE executives to tell him the unvarnished truth about their results and their business situation. Distorting facts or "spinning the numbers" when results fell short of expectations was absolutely forbidden. Welch demanded accountability for results, recognizing that blaming outside circumstances was a smoke screen, and that getting at the true causes of undesirable performance was the only way to stage powerful course corrections.

I invite you to treat the following set of questions as if you were reporting to Jack Welch. Don't just answer quietly to yourself, but actually take out a pencil and mark where you stand along the continuum beneath each question. This will provide a visual representation of where you have drawn the strategic line in the sand—closer to replicator (left side) or trendsetter (right side). Answer each question with ruthless honesty.

1. Look back five years and compare your strategic position then and now. Does the difference suggest that you have made minor tweaks, but have essentially lived the same year five times over? Or, when you compare your strategic position five years ago with today's, do you find your company unrecognizable?

   Minor tweaks...Unrecognizable

2. If your management team had a day-long meeting, which topic would they be able to discuss with greater ease: Topic A: Building more efficient cost saving processes, or Topic B: Novel ways for innovatively growing the business? Have you exhausted the possibility of getting leaner and meaner? Is it time to look to the top line and the objective of sales growth? Which of these labels best describes your management team?

   Efficiency experts..............Innovative growth strategists

3. What is the main intent of your strategy: Preserving the status quo in the marketplace? Playing catch-up with the industry's trendsetters? Preparing your organization for a market leadership position in the future?

   Status quo..Market leadership
   Playing catch-up................................Market leadership

4. If your competition got wind of your viewpoint about the marketplace of the future, would their reaction be boredom or would their jaws drop in surprise at the originality of your foresight?

   Ho-hum viewpoint...........................**Startling foresight**

5. Is your strategy development substantially a process of drawing upon conventional approaches endorsed by your industry, or is it about conceiving a new future that wouldn't ordinarily happen?

   Extrapolating from conventions...Envisioning new futures

6. Do you have distinct practices for identifying the needs of tomorrow's customers as opposed to how you determine the needs of today's customers?

   One set of practices........................**Different practices**

7. Where is the larger percentage of senior management's time invested—improving today's margins or producing a sustainable advantage?

   Improving margins.....**Producing sustainable advantage**

8. How do you work with future trend information? Is the information used to forecast the dominant future where your industry and market are heading? Or do you synthesize the trends to invent an original future that carries a strategically advantageous position in the marketplace?

   Forecasting industry's future.........**Inventing own future**

9. What scenario is considered riskier for your business: Being on the vanguard of change and running the risk of making a costly mistake? Or being slow and allowing your competition to be first to bring new value to the marketplace?

   Mistake avoidance...............................**Slow to innovate**

10. Is the major opportunity for innovative thinking largely confined to a strategic planning retreat? Does the opportunity for innovative thinking occur constantly, with the annual retreat becoming a time to formalize decisions regarding which innovations to pursue?

    Innovation treated as ritual.....**Constant innovative thinking**

11. Is your readiness for change based on waiting for clear evidence (handwriting on the wall) that your winning formula is used up? Or do you change proactively while you are still winning so that barely detectable signs of decline are nipped in the bud?

    Handwriting on the wall.................Maintain clean walls

12. When people discuss "differentiation," are they referring to comparing themselves against competitors on the traditional measures of value in your industry or are they pointing to creating differentiation that is hard to copy?

    Benchmarking well.....................................Hard to copy

13. What is your competitive posture—fighting to stay competitive in delivering the same basic value offering as your rivals or creating such distinctive innovations and market segmentation that competition is minimized?

    Fight to stay competitive....Innovate to minimize competition

14. Does your organization understand the different styles of thinking that are required in conversations about operational performance vs. strategic innovation? Does thinking occur on a whatever-comes-natural-to-the-participants basis or is it orchestrated to fit with the objectives being pursued in a given conversation or phase of planning?

    Undifferentiated thinking......Thinking tied to objective

15. Other than scheduling a strategic planning retreat, has your organization ever set out to systematically examine and describe its strategy process? Have you ever taken into account the conditions that lead to greater likelihood of conceiving bold innovations in contrast to strategic processes that virtually guarantee that past precedents will remain intact?

    Random process...........Process designed for innovation

Which questions stirred your strongest reactions of fear or pride or surprise? Notice the pattern of your responses. The closer your ratings were toward the right of the continuum, the more your business was on the trendsetter side of the line. If your assessments favored the left of the continuum, you were predominantly involved in a replicator strategy.

As a replicator, change represents the final curtain on a long-running play. The once-riveting script has lost its appeal to contemporary markets. In contrast, trendsetters are jubilant about the prospect of a never-ending sequence of opening nights, because they have learned how to create fresh innovations every time.

They know how to be the only one that does what they do.

Chapter

4

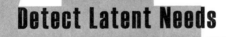

Detect Latent Needs

Detect Latent Needs

"Give your customers the ability to do what they can't do, but would have wanted to do, if they only knew they could have done it."

— Daniel Burris, Technology Futurist

When the stone tablets containing the Ten Commandments for Business Success come down from Corporate Mount Sinai, a "no-brainer" commandment will be: Give customers what they want. Whether the asking comes through focus groups, market research, suggestion boxes, or impromptu conversations at trade shows, careful listening to the expressed needs of customers is a highly revered factor in business success. In fact, losing touch with customer needs is viewed as a serious error and frightening prospect.

How do you give customers what they need but might never even think to ask for?

But customers aren't technology wizards, futurists, or visionaries. If you had asked farmers in the 1800s what they wanted, they would probably have answered, "A horse that's twice as strong and eats half as much." Most likely they wouldn't have replied, "How about making me a tractor?"

If you want to get ideas for improving a current product offering, take the traditional route of researching what customers want. But if you want explosive sales growth and sustainable advantage, you must do much more. You have to innovate and provide solutions for customers' latent needs—which brings us to Big Idea #3:

> **Big Idea #3: Give customers what they need but never thought to ask for.**

How do you go about detecting customer needs that may be so subliminal that they can't ever put them in words?

Detecting latent needs begins with having empathy for the customer's situation. Trendsetters spot frustrations that their customers have grown accustomed to and are now accommodating. While competitors may have the same facts about market trends, customer values, or buying behavior, trendsetters tease out original meaning and implications that suggest novel business opportunities.

They also possess the imagination for brainstorming out-of-the-box solutions that leave the customer wondering, "How did I live without this innovation?" This ability to work with latent needs requires substantially more skill than simply hearing customer requests and giving them exactly what they say they want.

Dangers of Giving Customers Only What They Say They Want

"We spent months asking the senior executives to spell out exactly what programs they wanted from us, " said a national accounts manager of a Fortune 100 consumer products company. "This warehouse club is an important account, and we were willing to invest our time and resources in giving them exactly what they told us. After a few months of preparing the exact solutions they requested, we shared them with the senior management team. When the presentation was done, they hardly said anything, but I took their nonverbals to mean, 'We're not impressed. What else have you got?'"

Before looking at ways to uncover latent needs, let's explore seven dangers that lurk within the standard practice of developing a business strategy based on responding to customers' articulated needs.

Danger #1: Expecting customers to come up with your innovations

When customers are invited to describe what they want, the majority request tweaks on current products and services—faster, cheaper, better. However, they provide little help when solicited for ideas that depart from what is familiar. Evaluating what is currently available requires a totally different style of thinking from imagining novel products and services. Accordingly, strategic planners must be realistic about what customers can and cannot contribute to their search for innovation.

Danger #2: Turning your customers into non-salaried decision makers

When strategic development is a "give-them-what-they-want" exercise, customers are actually being asked to contribute to the company strategy. Senior management is merely a rubber stamp for customers' preferences when too much significance is placed on customer requests. For example, if the customer satisfaction index shows a large percentage of "very satis-fied" ratings, replicators may decide that tweaking the current products and services will be sufficient. Data can also be used to fuel the argument against truly innovative ideas when the research doesn't suggest a sufficient market.

Don't get me wrong. The problem here isn't in gathering customer input, but in *how* the information is treated. Effective innovation uses cus-tomer input to stimulate corporate imagination, not to serve as the highest priority among strategic decision-making criteria. It is just one ingredient to throw into the creativity blender. That feedback should be synthesized with a rich mix of items, including futurists' plausible assumptions, employee insights, industry trend studies, demographic data, and value profiles of key market segments.

Danger #3: Focusing exclusively on established customers

Most would agree that solving the expressed needs of your ideal cli-ents is a sound course of action. Without question, chances of sustaining high margins are increased by working in markets where your brand is valued, your assets are already deployed, and decent profit margins already exist. Following this line of thinking, the marching orders dictate funneling resources, assembling strategic alliances, and structuring organizations to serve these markets.

However, such a strategy comes with a major vulnerability—no chance for exploiting new, minimally contested markets. Emerging markets are excluded, leaving new opportunities to be captured by nimble, nontraditional competitors. The lost opportunities in emergent markets, while initially less profitable, often become more lucrative than the mainstream market.

Danger #4: Going along with customers' capacity to accommodate

Let's admit it. Most of us can't imagine a totally new way of getting a particular job done until somebody implements a true innovation. People were satisfied with sending the kids over to the neighbors with messages, until the telephone was invented. Typewriters seemed pretty good, until we got word processing and computer spreadsheets. Postal service delivery was satisfactory until the advent of overnight mail, fax machines, and now e-mail. Do you think that anyone yearns for the days of feeding punch cards into mainframe computers?

Only when the next technological advance is unleashed do we become discontent with what is familiar. Customers have no idea that they have actually grown accustomed to a compromise.

Danger #5: Mistaking early rejection as a sign of innovation failure

Innovative organizations are prepared for customers to reject eventual blockbuster products during their introduction. Twenty years ago, phonograph record turntable users rejected CD players. Automated teller machines were thought to be depersonalizing banking. Currently, only the early adopters of innovation are actively using on-board navigation in cars. In fact, immediate market acceptance of a new product or service is often a danger sign that the envelope of orthodoxy hasn't been pushed far enough.

Danger #6: Tolerating customers' lethargic pace of technological change

"Our company is 110 years old and serves 30,000 retailers of mostly family-owned stores," said a wholesale food service executive. "Ninety percent of them don't own a computer, so we are constrained by our customers' unwillingness to innovate."

This wholesaler could be waiting an awfully long time for his retail operators to request technological upgrades. The risk of serving technologically antiquated customers is that sooner or later you will go out of business along with them. The only viable choice is to become a catalyst for innovation. A core competence in innovation introduction is a prerequisite for being a trendsetter in serving a change-resistant market.

Danger # 7: Asking today's customers about future customers.

It's one thing to know what customers want today, but quite another to know what they'll yearn for in five years. When I ask marketers, "How do you learn about today's customers' needs?" they reply, "Suggestion boxes, focus groups, and customer satisfaction surveys." My next question is, "How do you anticipate your future customer's needs?" Before they reply with the same answer—suggestion boxes, focus groups, and customer satisfaction surveys—they sheepishly catch on to the flaw in their methodology. How do we expect to use the same information gathering approaches and yet expect different needs to show up between today's and tomorrow's customers?

When you are aiming for a sustainable competitive advantage, the practice of giving customers only what they say they want is a dangerous one. Anticipating customer needs requires a different brand of thinking than simply listening to literal suggestions and complaints, and rendering obvious solutions. Trendsetters are distinguished by their uncanny ability to recognize needs at the "level of a whisper."

Listening to the Whisper

Nearly all conversation between service providers and their customers centers around expressed or articulated needs. But the greatest potential for triggering innovations that no one else can imagine comes from going beyond the chatter of articulated needs, to sense the whisper of latent needs.

The term "whisper" refers to the implied wishes, hidden dreams, and unrecognized accommodations of customers.

There are two types of whispers. The first whisper occurs when customers feel an inkling of a need that they can't quite express. But once a trendsetter provides them with the ability to do what they can't do currently, the innovation becomes a necessity.

The second type of whisper occurs when customers know what is needed but don't have anyone to offer a solution. Either there is no service provider, or those available aren't offering an important element of value, like quality, speed, or convenience.

Let's consider examples of both types of whispers.

Ed Bradley, correspondent for *60 Minutes*, went to Finland to uncover how, in perhaps the shyest country in the world, Nokia managed to sell wireless phones to 60 percent of the adult population (compared to 25 percent in the United States) and to nearly 100 percent of the teenage population. On the surface, there was no sense in targeting shy people as a market segment for communication devices.

An innovation catalyst, Nokia figured out how to address the subtle communication needs that shy people were unlikely to express. First, Nokia recognized that wireless communication reduced the risks of the intimacy involved in eye contact, facial gestures, and non-verbal expressions. In addition, the text-messaging feature didn't betray strong emotions, so adolescents, for example, could type, "I like you" without the embarrassment of uncomfortable pauses or stammering. Finally, wireless phones allowed teenagers the freedom to roam and call friends without the fear of being overheard by parents. By detecting latent needs, Nokia recognized that shy people would be big fans of private, non-emotional communication devices. They cornered the Finnish market.

Alert entrepreneurs always have their antennae activated to detect obvious frustrations that have no apparent solution. For instance, Bruce Merrel, CEO of Laptop Lane, conceived his business while observing an expensively attired executive on his hands and knees at the airport, scouring for an outlet to plug in his computer. He also noticed three trends: an increase in the number of business travelers, more of them carrying laptops, and many of them expecting to stay in constant touch with colleagues and customers. Merrill concluded that corporate travelers had an unfulfilled need for communications support while on the road. In response, he set up comfortable, full service workstations at airports that included copying, overnight shipping, conference room rentals, fax machines, and printers. Each location has four to 12 offices, all 36-48 square feet, with 7-foot high walls. Renting space costs $2 for the first five minutes, and 38 cents for each additional minute, including local and long-distance phone calls and faxes.

How to Tease Out Latent Needs

Imagine Memphis in the 1950s. Teenaged girls used to swarm around the house of Elvis Presley, plucking precious blades of grass from his lawn. Like multitudes of others, Elvis' manager, Colonel Tom Parker, marveled at this amazing gesture of adoration. But *un*like any others, he saw an opportunity in his observation. He realized that if Elvis' fans would pick his grass, they'd buy clothing, dolls, lunch boxes, movies, and just about anything imprinted with his identity. What they yearned for was a tangible keepsake that would connect and bond them with their idol.

The marketing genius of Colonel Parker illustrates the most indispensable talent of trendsetters: their extraordinary capacity to go beyond obvious observations of customers or survey numbers and interpret implicit desires. Since, by definition, latent needs are not obvious, how do you develop the ability to recognize them? Let's follow in the footsteps of a few successful innovators and study their best techniques.

Listen to customers in the midst of a service experience

Strategist Kenichi Ohmae wrote in the *Harvard Business Review*, "Personally, I would much rather talk with three housewives for two hours each on their feelings about, say, washing machines, than conduct a 1,000-person survey on the same topic. I get much better insight and perspective on what they are really looking for."

A growing number of strategists agree with Ohmae. Analytic market research is especially useful in testing customer reactions to early product prototypes. When the goal is generating unusual customer insights, nothing beats live interviews, especially in the actual place of service delivery.

Harbor Properties CEO Robert Holmes and his team at Stevens Pass Ski Resort came to understand the importance of one-on-one listening for teasing out latent needs. Holmes had noticed that traditional surveys typically yielded the same two answers. When asked what they wanted, skiers said, "More ski lifts." When asked what bugged them, they replied, "High lift ticket prices."

Not satisfied with these routine responses, Stevens Pass now holds interviews just about anywhere and anytime. While riding on chairlifts, unloading equipment from cars, or helping skiers having trouble getting off the lifts, interviewers ask questions like: What do you like about the season pass? What would you like to see added to it? How would you handle the problem you just told me about?

The idea for a weekday season pass resulted from these interviews. With the slopes already packed on winter weekends, Stevens developed a special reduced-rate season pass for off-peak times. In its first offering, Stevens Pass sold 6,500 weekday season ski passes.

If you can interview on a ski slope, why not in a bank lobby, a warehouse loading dock, or the home office of a user downloading a software program? Observing and listening for latent needs in the midst of the actual service experience yields very different responses than those from some focus group assembled in a hotel meeting room.

Treat complaints as an implied wish list

Complaints are a wonderful way to learn about latent needs. There are two major kinds of complaints, those about unacceptable performance, and those that reveal latent needs. When faced with the former, don't probe for deeper needs, just correct the mistake.

The second kind of complaint is very different. When customers say in a cranky tone, "Why can't you guys do this?" they are actually revealing a void in service that no company seems to be addressing. This complaint is actually a wonderful opportunity.

Take the situation of one of my clients, Federal Express. After I explained the concept of latent needs to him, a general manager said to me, "We're actually hearing customers complain about having deliveries come to their mailroom. They want to eliminate the mailroom and have all packages and letters be dropped off at their desks."

Now Fed Ex might treat this wish as outrageous, impractical, and too costly. But, as the manager confided, "What if we ignore this wish, but one of our competitors takes it seriously, and solves the apparent logistical problem? Where does that leave us?"

If no solution to the complainer's problem currently exists, then the first company to devise an effective resolution is sitting on a potential goldmine.

Replicators hear this type of complaint and dismiss it with comments like: "I've never heard that before," or, "Here's why we can't do that." In contrast, trendsetters listen and look for answers to these original requests.

One of my clients actually encourages his employees to maintain a "why can't you give us this" complaint log. Every quarter this implied wish list is given to the best people in the organization to orchestrate a solution. For instance, new product complaints are circulated to R&D, marketing, and engineering. New service complaints are dispatched to operations. And all complaints are sent to senior management so they gain a cumulative sense of available new business opportunities. Whether senior management chooses to act on one, 10, or zero items on the complaints list is of secondary importance. The point of this practice is to get creative juices stirred up by the chance to address the implied wishes underlying complaints.

Be alert to compromises

In a compromise, both customers and their service providers can't hear the whispers of discontent or the desire for improved performance imbedded in the situation. Cab drivers don't accept credit cards, and passengers don't expect them to. Airlines can't seem to get special-meal orders correct, so the flight attendants expect passengers to humbly accept the standard offering of chicken or pasta without complaint. Patients with appointments are left to cool their heels in waiting rooms with no recourse because, after all, the doctor, whose time is so precious, is busy with other patients. Medical practitioners don't even perceive what a turn-off the term "waiting room" is!

Can you see the opportunity in offering solutions to customers who routinely accept compromises? Service providers who are replicators don't notice a problem or don't care enough to seek a cost-effective solution. In contrast, trendsetters are intrigued by the enormous profit potential in being first to address areas of customer compromise.

Consider the mail order catalog operator Travel Smith. My wife and I became aware of their unique products while preparing for a trip to Chile. We like to balance our vacation time hiking in scenic backwoods settings, touring historic sites, and dining in upscale restaurants. But our varied itineraries often create wardrobe dilemmas. Carrying enough clothing to accommodate such varied activities would mean extra luggage, giving the airlines that many more bags to "misplace." But, if we pack lightly, we face the unpleasant prospect of washing and ironing our garments or sending them out for laundering at virtually every stop.

Travel Smith's catalog is filled with a large assortment of sports coats, shirts, slacks, and exercise attire in special fast-drying, wrinkle-resistant fabric. Our clothing can be washed in a hotel sink, hung up to dry, and be ready to wear the next morning without ironing. Travel Smith provides solutions that eliminate the usual compromises of active travelers.

Aspiring business innovators can start to hone their skills by cultivating the ability to spot compromises in situations like dining out, vacationing, shopping, commuting to work, and doing home maintenance. Train your mind to see compromises in your daily life, and you can transfer the skill to your business.

Here are a few of the items found on my list of compromises:

- No receptionist to answer phones at doctors' offices between noon and 2 p.m.
- Electric shavers that scrape and pull at your face.
- Milk at the back of the grocery store instead of the front, where you could run in and pick it up quickly.
- Doctors who won't communicate their diagnoses or recommendations with families of senior citizens who can't remember the information themselves.
- The tech support runaround where the software provider says, "That's not our problem, it's a hardware problem," and the hardware guy says, "Not us, call your software provider."
- Airlines' low rate of delivering special meal orders.
- Taxis that don't take credit cards.
- Cell phone services that claim to offer national coverage, but try making a call on your road trip through Montana or Wyoming.
- Hospital bills you can't understand.
- Never knowing how to accurately compare the long distance rates of telephone companies.

Being alert to compromise in your own life will help you develop the practice of noticing frustrations customers may be having with your company's service or products. This practice will bring you closer to discovering their latent needs.

Even Mature Markets Offer Exciting Opportunities

The ability to detect latent needs and package effective solutions to them even transforms so-called mature markets into thriving business opportunities.

In the 1960s, how many people do you think were asking their doctors for a "wellness program?" Dr. Kenneth Cooper, founder of aerobic exercise, pioneered the new field of wellness while most physicians were confining their practices to treating disease and illness, thereby restricting the market's potential. Accordingly, consumers sought services only when their symptoms reached the point of "being sick enough to see a doctor."

Dr. Cooper's innovations arose from two insights. The first involved logic that was radical for its time: Preventing the onset of disease is cheaper and more effective than treating illness. Cooper's second insight required reading the implicit wishes of a certain segment of the population—people who wanted to maintain their bodies at optimum health. Their problem was the lack of sound medical expertise to help them reach their lofty fitness goals.

Cooper's groundbreaking research used Air Force trainees in San Antonio, Texas, as subjects. He analyzed which exercise regimens produced the most beneficial fitness levels and desired health benefits. His findings were revolutionary at the time, as some doctors were actually questioning whether exercise might *endanger* patients' health. The results were published in the book, *Aerobics*, which became an instant best seller. The Cooper Aerobics Center rapidly acquired a year-long membership waiting list at its workout facility.

By providing an ideal vision of health care service, Cooper helped unearth a new market niche of fitness enthusiasts. While mainstream medical practitioners ignored a latent need, consumers ran (literally) to reap the benefits of wellness programs.

In the mid-1970s, the market for wellness services seemed to peak, especially among prospective customers turned off by its "no pain, no gain" intensity. The Fitness Revolution became a lost cause for the watching-on-the-sidelines market segment that complained, "Exercise may be good for me, but why does it have to be such hard work? Can't it be more fun?"

Perhaps the best solution to the need for fun came from the developers of dance exercise. Pioneered by Jackie Sorenson and Judy

Shepherd-Misset of Jazzercise, Inc., this exercise form fulfilled the "fun" requirement—inspiring aerobic dance instructors, motivating class environment, and rocking to upbeat music. Once again, new value (fun) generated a flurry of spin-off products and services, including aerobic dance studios, exercise attire in leotards and shoes, instructional videos, books and specialized magazines, water bottles, and sports drinks.

The originators of dance exercise looked to the unserved niche of fun-seeking exercisers as a signal to address their compromise. Exercise could be fun.

Capitalizing on Cooper's original premise—it is cheaper and more effective to prevent disease than to treat it—a new wave of innovation catalysts packaged corporate wellness programs to curb rising employer health care costs. After exhausting their search to find low-cost health insurers, progressive companies realized the best way to reduce expenses was to have healthier employees. Corporate wellness programs bundled a broad range of services, including health risk appraisals, fitness testing, organizational stress studies, and employee assistance programs. The expansion to a full array of wellness services suited to the emerging corporate market illustrates the effectiveness of looking beyond the original method of distribution (wellness services packaged for individual consumers) to places where a similar product is likely to be attractive (corporations).

The sequence of market rejuvenations of the wellness industry questions the very notion of mature markets. In reality, market maturity is more a matter of the entrenched thinking of industry incumbents than anything specific about the market. Rather than adopting a combative steal-market-share strategy, trendsetters follow the clues to uncovering latent needs. Their innovations inject fresh, compelling value that stimulates sales growth.

The Power of Looking Beneath the Surface

Looking back with hindsight on trendsetter innovations, it is tempting to wonder why other industry players didn't see the same opportunity. How could so many have missed out? This leads us to what happens when Big Idea #3 is ignored. Companies that can't or won't tease out latent customer needs fail to detect new business opportunities. Few are willing to cultivate the quality of thinking that produces business opportunities no one else can imagine.

Having laid the groundwork for understanding the concept of latent needs, the next step involves learning how to systematically reconceive data, observations, and bits of knowledge so they are more likely to become wealth-generating ideas. Chapter 5 presents unusual vantage points from which to spot latent needs and develop solutions. In Chapter 6, we will examine the insightful types of questions that occupy the minds of visionaries when they are conceiving fruitful business opportunities.

Chapter

5

Fresh Eyes

Chapter

5 Fresh Eyes

"There is only one way to see things
until someone shows us how to see them with different eyes."
—Pablo Picasso

O ne of the most memorable sporting events I have ever attended occurred in Seattle's Kingdome in 1996. My wife, Haley, and I were watching our first-ever baseball game together. Pitching for the Seattle Mariners was Randy Johnson, the tallest pitcher in baseball—6 feet 10 inches—and, with his 100 mph fastball, one of the most formidable.

Johnson struck out eight of the first 10 Oakland A's batters. Early on, I sensed we might be witnessing a record-setting performance for strikeouts in a single game. Nor was I the only one entertaining this possibility. At every two-strike count, 50,000 fans rose from their seats to cheer Johnson on to pump strike three past the hitter.

What are the best out-of-the-box thinking methods for conceiving novel business opportunities?

Flush with enthusiasm, I shouted to Haley, "Isn't this incredible?"

"I'm glad we're standing up so much," she yelled back, "This game is a real snoozer—nothing's happening."

"Nothing's happening?" I was stunned. "The pitcher is going for a record."

"If that guy is so good, why can't he throw the ball so the batter can hit it? He's ruining everyone's chance to run, chase the ball, throw it, and slide across the bases. Isn't this a spectator sport? The way he's pitching, nobody is doing squat."

In that moment, Haley had reconceived baseball, transforming it from a win-lose game where strikeouts are good, to a sport whose goal is to create the most action for the spectators. Haley has two Masters degrees, but in her 39 years on planet Earth, no one had ever briefed her about the rules of baseball. Precisely because she was ignorant of the rules, she could view the game with fresh eyes and perceive the action on the field in an original way, vastly different, of course, from that of the other 50,000 knowledgeable baseball fans.

Unlike baseball, business doesn't have a rulebook with umpires on the field, except perhaps in the case of government regulations. The rules in business really amount to tacit understandings, where industry members substantially agree about what constitutes markets, competition, customers, methods of distribution, margins, and even what to measure. Every aspect of a business is covered. While these "agreed upon" rules summarize how businesses have operated in the past, they limit what we see, what we aspire to, and the scope of our imagination.

Chapter Five was written to help you regain your capacity to look at your business with fresh eyes, even if you are a 39-year industry veteran. The best way to read it is with the same blindness Haley brought to watching baseball. I invite you to transcend the conventions you know so well and master Big Idea #4:

> **Big Idea #4: Observe the familiar with fresh eyes.**

Seeing out of the box

Every bold innovation comes from a fresh way of seeing—a shift of focus. The freshness is not in the pure sense of sight, but in the original thinking applied to what is seen. It is not simply a matter of *what* you know, but the style of thinking you impose upon what you know. To create a truly innovative strategy, you must be able to reconceive familiar phenomena.

Take coffins for example. What better place to illustrate out-of-the-box thinking than by looking at an industry that manufactures the rectangular wooden box we all recognize as a coffin? In the name of new product development, can you fathom a line of "designer coffins?"

Well, someone did. While perusing exhibits at the Seattle Art Museum, I turned into a new alcove, and there before my eyes was a coffin in the shape of a Mercedes Benz.

This product innovation began in the 1970s in Ghana, when a fisherman approached the apprentice carpenter, Kene Kwei, with an unusual request. He wanted a coffin made in the shape of a fish. Being customer-friendly, Kwei complied, which quickly triggered a flurry of similar customer requests. A boxer was buried in a sneaker-shaped coffin. A hunter's coffin was shaped like a lion. And the wealthy owner of a fleet of taxis got the Mercedes Benz. Customers who preferred a church memorial service used Bible-shaped coffins.

How could such a break from centuries-old precedent gain rapid market acceptance? The designer coffins addressed a latent need. West Africans believe that reincarnation occurs within a nuclear family provided the deceased is impressed with the funeral and burial ceremonies. The lavish coffins glorify their life achievements.

If the shape of a coffin is up for grabs, what about the "box" in which you hold your business? Why not entertain the ideas that come from viewing the familiar with fresh eyes, and open up an array of opportunities?

Tired Eyes vs. Fresh Eyes

In an age of unprecedented information accessibility, it is unlikely that any company can hoard exclusive marketplace information long enough to produce an enduring competitive edge. An advantage doesn't come from the information itself, but how strategists interpret the information. Replicators process information with "tired eyes"—they take well-known information and draw the same conclusions as everyone else.

The future is not proprietary. But an organization's perspective about the future can be. When your perspective becomes the envy of almost everyone else in your industry, you get acknowledged as a visionary trendsetter.

Are there methods to increase the likelihood of shifts of focus so they happen by design? Are there ways to develop fresh perspectives that will make you an acknowledged trendsetter and the envy of others in your industry?

Let's look at seven "fresh-eye" perspectives that can stimulate breathtaking imagination.

Clear Eyes See the Obvious

How do you look at your business with fresh eyes when you have worked in an industry for decades? Start by understanding that our assumptions about how a business should be run are not the Truth. Industry members substantially agree on the effectiveness of these assumptions, so they are accepted without question. These assumptions tell us the business basics: roles to hire for, expected profit margins, merchandizing to include in a store, departments to include on the organizational chart, and virtually every detail about running a business.

Unfortunately, we don't notice how these assumptions affect what we see, how we analyze decisions, and ultimately, what we do. The advantage of using a "clear-eyes" perspective is that we get to see a facet of our reality that others can't see, even though it is right in front of them.

At first glance, it seems unlikely that any kind of brilliant insights can result from simply describing objective reality or making explicit what most everyone presumes to be true. Where's the freshness? The illogical truth is that dissecting the intricacies of a business or industry's workings can open the floodgates for creative genius to emerge.

Before you can think outside the box, you have to know what's *in* the box. As long as the box remains largely invisible, there is little chance to enlarge or alter our thinking. This is why I use the term "tired eyes" to describe being lodged in the box of conventional thinking. By jolting the unexamined notions of how a business is supposed to operate, the rigidity of the box weakens, and the initial dimensions of possibility defined by the box are expanded. Dramatic shifts of focus can occur only when we treat the box as a mental construction that contains our assumptions—not necessarily the Truth—one deserving frequent re-examinations in ever-changing times.

The perspective of an observational comic

Two groups that have mastered the ability to point out life's obvious imbedded assumptions are comedians and social commentators.

Jerry Seinfeld, talking about coffins, wonders, "Why do they give pillows to dead people?"

And Andy Rooney of *60 Minutes* comments, "Are the soap-dish manufacturers paying off the people who build soap dishes into showers? If they aren't, how come the soap holders are always placed so they take a direct hit from the shower water? Then, for the rest of the day, the soap just sits there dissolving in a puddle of water."

Or, as a recent e-mail I received noted: "Only in America do we leave cars worth thousands of dollars in the driveway and leave useless things and junk in boxes in the garage. Only in America, do people order double cheeseburgers, a large order of French fries...and a Diet Coke."

Scott Adams, creator of the best-selling *Dilbert* series, pokes fun at the ridiculous things transpiring at work. It's hard to believe that Adam's examples convey real experiences, but the scary/depressing part is that his books wouldn't sell if the stories didn't ring true.

The common ingredient of observational comics is their skill in looking at the everyday experiences that everybody else glosses over, which, when revealed in bold relief, show the contradictions and sheer silliness of our routines. The humor lies in stirring the surprising audience recognition, "I never saw it that way, but now that I do, that's really funny." Being able to shine a verbal spotlight on the concealed humor in unnoticed daily routines requires extraordinary observational skills.

The observational comic clearly describes "what's so" about daily routines, and in the next instant, scans to see "what's silly or ridiculous in that familiar scene?" Similarly, once businesspeople adopt a "clear-eye" vantage point, they notice standard business practices and assumptions, and then have a perspective from which to imagine, "What would it look like to go against the grain of convention?"

How to view current reality with clear eyes

What are your industry's beliefs and assumptions about how business should be done? In addressing this question, take the viewpoint of a comedian who knows nothing about the inner workings of your industry but is intent on observing how things get done. Write down your industry's assumptions.

Here is a sample list for a hypothetical industry:

- While customers might tell you they want service and quality products, the main thing they want is low price.
- The best way to make money is by buying smart and capitalizing on volume buying deals.
- Wages should be kept within 30 cents of the legislated minimum.
- The checkout area of a store should display impulse-buy items.
- Summer is a slow time of year for sales in this industry.

Every business move reflects an explicit or implicit assumption. The goal is to categorize both types of assumptions in a way that empowers you to innovate. Sort the items on your list of assumptions into the following three categories:

1. Things that you know are likely to remain effective in furthering business goals. These are keepers.
2. Things that you know are no longer so. These need to be discarded.

3.   Things that you are unsure of—that require further thought. Question these to determine their current accuracy and effectiveness.

This exercise develops observational skills for describing implicit industry rules and treating them with appropriate suspicion. Having this capacity sets you up to dismantle the assumptions that preserve the past, and to begin to view your business with the "fresh-eye" vantage points that follow.

Contrarian Eyes Swim Upstream

Contrarians challenge the implicit common sense of an industry. As rebellious thinkers, they watch what everyone else does and then do the opposite. When ideas trigger massive skepticism, contrarians suspect they might be worth pursuing.

With a preference to go against the grain, contrarians disdain formal rules imposed by government or other sanctioning bodies. Think of Henry Ford experimenting with the prototype automobile before regulators even had a chance to consider issuing driver's licenses. Think of Dallas Cowboys' owner Jerry Jones who, in contempt of National Football League rules, signed his own deals with Nike and Coca-Cola.

To a contrarian, a deregulated industry is like a candy store to an unsupervised kid. To a replicator, deregulation creates the unnerving chaos that comes with having to ward off new competition.

Not your mother's grocery store: A retailing contrarian

Orchestral music serenaded me as I drove up to the Admiral Thriftway Supermarket in West Seattle. Terry Halverson, owner of this three-store chain, greeted me and we set out on a tour of his establishment.

In the center of the store, I was caught off guard by the bustle of activity in The Kiosk. In front of an oven, a stove, cooking oils, wines, and pots and pans, demonstrators prepared recipes that could be completed in 15 minutes or less. The Kiosk schedule for the week was posted on a black-board, so customers could plan their shopping trips at a time when they could learn a particular recipe and taste the finished dish.

When asked how he could afford the cost of preparing and giving away so many samples, Terry noted, "While most chains and independents believe cost cutting is the best way to stretch margins, I believe you've got to spend money to make money. Whatever we spend on The Kiosk, we make back in spades. Products demonstrated there fly off the shelves."

When we got to the checkout area, I was in for another surprise. Familiar with the merchandising strategy of using the front end of the store for impulse buys, I expected to see the *National Enquirer*, Wrigley's spear-mint gum, Gillette razor blades, or Snickers bars. Instead I saw *Bon Appetite*, *Martha Stewart Living*, fine chocolates imported from France, exotic salsas, oils, and other specialty products. What could Terry have been thinking by putting expensive items up front?

"Where else in the store do customers pause for a few minutes and actually have the time to get educated about award-winning upscale products that give us higher margins?" he explained.

Strolling over to the bakery, I was blown away by a sign bearing the words, "Fresh bread from Paris every Friday morning." Admiral Thriftway is the only supermarket in the country that imports that signature product.

I was still trying to figure out where Terry skimped to cover costs. Maybe with the biggest cost of all—personnel? Not so. I discovered a certified nutritionist and respiratory therapist in the Nutrition Department. She was educating shoppers about herbs and supplements, product categories where national sales are soaring because of the growing aging population. Terry Halverson had the "cents" to prove that when a dedicated professional works the nutrition department, revenues far exceed self-service. Terry was violating that old retailing axiom: The best way to curb labor costs is to have plenty of part-timers and self-service departments.

Admiral Thriftway doesn't operate in an upscale neighborhood; the demographics are middle-class, at best. Terry contends that he would put this store design in lots of neighborhoods with varying economic status.

"While the rich sink their discretionary cash into new cars, boats, and vacations, people with fewer financial resources invest in special foods and delicacies. Most of my colleagues don't see it that way," he said.

Most other grocery stores don't approach his sales figures either. Admiral Thriftway's sales-per-square-foot are twice the average for members of its retailing cooperative.

Terry Halverson is a maverick retailer. Not only does he operate with contrarian eyes, but he also has the guts to assume the risks of innovation. In the words of one of his respectful competitors, "Terry is willing to bite the bullet longer than the rest of us."

How to think like a contrarian

Go back to the three categories of assumptions you prepared in the "Clear Eyes" exercise. For the items in the third category "unsure of—requiring further thought," describe how doing the opposite of the assumption would look. One of my clients, a convenience store distributor, wrote these assumptions: "The target customer for convenience stores is an 18- to 35-year-old male, mid- to low-income status, without a college degree. The profit centers of a convenience store are gasoline, limited assortment groceries, cigarettes, beverages (especially beer), and a car wash."

As contrarians, they then designed a revolutionary convenience store for career women ages 25 to 45, of middle- to upper- income status. Obviously, a very different definition of convenience is present for a population of extremely busy people who aren't rich enough to afford household managers, maids, chefs, drivers, and personal assistants. Yet, they still want time to kick back and read a novel, or bake brownies with their kids.

Their group pondered the question, "What would be on the to-do list of these career women that they'd love to delegate to an affordable resource?" This list of items from their flip chart suggested a number of convenience services, such as:

- A repair center for broken vacuum cleaners and televisions.
  We pick up the appliance and either do the repair, or outsource it to a qualified specialist.

- A ticket service for theater and sporting events.
- A fleet of cars to run errands. We buy your groceries, pick up dry cleaning, return overdue library books and home videos, drop off UPS packages, and pick up your car for servicing at the dealership. When you have large objects that won't fit into the garbage and needs to be taken to the dump, we'll send over a truck.
- A communications center for dealing with other vendors. We settle bill disputes, wait for repairmen to show up, and locate the hard-to-find resource (i.e., who are you going to call to find a bulletproof vest for your business client who loves to watch police dramas on television?).
- Meal preparation service. We offer meals for school lunches and for work, plus meal solutions for supper.

The group considered offering the service in two formats—to individual consumers and to corporations who want to offer the service as a perk to employees. By using contrarian eyes to redefine the traditionally targeted customer, the traditional convenience store is transformed into a lifestyle solutions center.

Collect about a dozen program brochures from your industry's most prestigious conferences. Develop a list of the topics frequently covered in the educational sessions. Then design your own conference topics on subjects no one else in the industry is talking about. For instance, instead of a typical program on employee retention that details fringe benefits and bonus packages, your conference could feature a session titled: "Designing a workplace where people would be willing to work for free."

Naive Eyes Ask Impossible Questions

Young children have a vivid, anything-is-possible viewpoint. Because they lack experience to know any better, kids aren't constrained by considerations of what is possible or impossible, what is realistic or unrealistic. Out of their innocence, they ask what more knowledgeable people might judge to be ridiculous or even stupid questions. Kids naturally bring naive eyes to their experience of life unfolding, and operate free of the restraints of limits, predictability, and past precedent.

In the game of innovative thinking, adults suffer from an overly serious reverence for precedents. This compulsion to replicate the past and go with the flow often arises from the need to be smart or at least appear smart. "Smartness" equates to having ready-made answers that have worked in the past. But this type of smartness comes with a built-in limitation. The more answers you possess, the less imaginative capacity you have to experiment, to explore the novel, and to expand the parameters of possibility.

As adults, we can't tolerate the position, "I don't know," and just exist in the psychological state of uncertainty.

Operating with naive eyes requires suspending judgments about what is realistic or unrealistic, and responding openly to any conceivable idea. Naive eyes are not exclusively reserved for children. Adults can ask outrageous questions, too. Why can't a homebuyer search a national video listing of homes for sale to tour the rooms and grounds online? Why can't electronic books be delivered to our computers on demand? Why can't we eliminate traffic jams around morning and evening rush hours? If we can give verbal commands to telephones, why can't we do the same with television sets and get rid of the TV channel clickers we can never find anyway?

While adults are capable of asking unusual questions, the desire to appear smart overrides that potential. As Peter Senge said, "To be a real learner is to be ignorant and incompetent. Not many top executives are up to that."

But true trendsetters know the power of ignorance. Take Wal-Mart's rise from a so-so to powerful player in the food industry. Fully Clingman, COO of the HEB supermarket chain, told an audience of marketing and advertising professionals, "Wal-Mart is successful because they keep asking dumb questions. They ask supply channel members, 'Why can't you do things in a different way?' questions that experienced supermarket retailers would never think to ask." Could ignorance of industry conventions be Wal-Mart's dominant competitive advantage?

Wal-Mart's ignorance of conventional retailing wisdom began long before they started selling food, with the basic philosophy of founder Sam Walton:

"Swim upstream. Go the other way. Ignore the conventional wisdom. If everybody else is doing it one way, there's a good chance you can find your niche by going in the exact opposite direction. But be prepared for a lot of folks to wave you down and tell you you're headed the wrong way. I guess in all my years, what I heard more often than anything was: A town of less than 50,000 population cannot support a discount store for very long."

In the 1960's, retailing wisdom dictated that mass merchandisers should locate stores in densely populated areas to generate sufficient sales volume. Having naive eyes, Wal-Mart did the opposite. They located their stores in small towns where extraordinary selection of top branded products at low prices enticed people to drive long distances to shop their stores. By not knowing any better, Wal-Mart ended up with thousands of stores without any head-to-head competition from a retailer of similar stature.

Decades back, retailers refrained from sharing point of sale figures, engaging in systems integration, or coordinating plans with manufacturers. Wal-Mart broke the rules by wondering, "If we're both serving the same customer, doesn't it make sense that we coordinate our efforts?" Consequently, they pioneered a strategic alliance with Proctor & Gamble featuring electronic transmission of point of sale data to the manufacturer's warehouse. This technological linkage permits just-in-time deliveries, thereby reducing inventory and decreasing labor costs associated with processing transactions. Wal-Mart strips costs out of the supply channel to lower their pricing. Meanwhile, most food retailers engage in forward buying of large volumes to lower their purchase costs with manufacturers, but end up carrying more expensive inventory. While the grocery industry took aggressive action in the 1980s to reduce supply channel costs, Wal-Mart operates with expense rates that competitors aren't likely to approach anytime soon.

Ignorance of the rules has paid off. In their first 36 years of operation, Wal-Mart, Wal-Mart Super Centers, and Sam's Clubs combined to capture 15 percent of the total U.S. retail market, including autos!

Long standing businesses must get ignorant in order to get smart—ignorant in the sense of never treating the industry's conventional wisdom as unquestionable dogma. The trendsetters' only dogma is: Question everything.

How to get ignorant to become smart

- Walk through your office, store, or plant, as you have never done before. Each step of the way; adopt the naive eyes of a young child and ask questions like, "Why are things done this way?" or "Why can't we do that a different way?"
- As you talk with manufacturers and distributors in your supply channel, notice the compromises being tolerated out of "it's-always-been-done-this-way" habit. Then imagine you are a child who feels no need to compromise. (Remember, kids don't care about budgets, so don't shut down your capacity for no-limit thinking at the very outset with preoccupations about paying for the innovation.)
- Better still, invite a group of grade-schoolers to tour your business and encourage them to voice their questions and share their reactions. Get ready for an eye-opening experience.

  In 1966, Payless Shoes President Maxine Clark left to pursue her mission of bringing the theater back to retailing. In her research, Clark visited a factory that offered tours to grade schools and scout troops. She observed how the process of seeing products actually being manufactured enthralled the children. Clark decided to recreate the factory's process in a mall-based retail experience, known as Build-A-Bear Workshop. The workshop is organized into a sequence of eight stations where children and adults work on their furry friend selected from 30 stuffed animals. The stations are titled Choose Me, Stuff Me, Hear Me (a record your own message chip to serve as the bear's voice), Stitch me, Fluff Me, Name Me (a birth certificate and entry into a bear tracking system), Dress Me, and Take Me Home (a carrying/storage case).

Clark's advisory board includes children ages six through 14. She is constantly checking ideas with friends' children, children she meets during travel, and of course, feedback from in-store questionnaires.

Build-A-Bear Workshop is one of the few mall-based interactive retailing experiences for children. In 1991, National Retail Federation honored the company with its Retail Innovator of the Year Award.

- Practice thinking like a kid who doesn't know any better. Pretend that you are a 6-year-old blessed with a huge capacity for no-limit thinking. What are the wildest dreams for services that you would love to have available? For example:

  - Why can't they develop some surgical procedure, neuron stimulation method, or drug to create selective memory, so we vividly recall happy times and totally forget unpleasant experiences?

  - While golfing, why can't we channel to our conscious minds the same thoughts Tiger Woods does when he contemplates a 12-foot putt?

  - Why can't we have a company that specializes in cleaning and organizing garages (so we can actually park our cars in them)?

  - Why can't there be an emergency number to call when you need help with a computer problem and you receive the tech support runaround?

- Why can't we create a commuting system that puts an end to traffic jams?
- Why can't some company create a single plastic card to store *all* my data so I don't have to carry a bulging wallet with five airline cards, three credit cards, two phone cards, and a health insurance card?
- Why can't we have personal submarines?
- Borrowing an idea from Star Trek, I wonder why we can't have a means for transporting matter through teleportation?
- Why can't we have a device that would convert our vocal tone so at any given moment we can sound like James Earl Jones, or Barbra Streisand?
- Why can't I be paid a commission every time my personal information is transferred from one company's database to another's?
- Why can't we have an electronic shopping service where you could input your shopping criteria for buying a product (a car that seats five comfortably, less than $35,000, etc.) and your PC would search through databases and produce an answer within an hour?
- Why can't we have an electronic gatekeeper to scan phone calls, voice mails, faxes, and e-mails based on a priority code that you could program into the system?

•••

Don't dismiss the business practicality of this exercise. Remember, Mark Cuban asked one single question, "What would it take to get Indiana Hoosier basketball broadcasts piped to Dallas?" How's that for thinking like a kid who didn't know any better back in 1994? That question brought radio to the Internet when Cuban founded AudioNet, which later sold as Broadcast.com for $2.4 billion in Yahoo! stock.

Wandering Eyes Discard Industry Boundaries

Wandering eyes look beyond industry rivals to products and services in other industries. They notice the tradeoffs customers make across substitute industries and recognize the opportunity in them.

The beauty of this approach lies in escaping a head-to-head competitive view of an industry. When strategizing is a knee-jerk reaction to the big players' strengths and weaknesses, nothing revolutionary emerges. Whether the eventual strategy is to match or beat a rival, it is likely to be bracketed within a common set of tacit understandings. When strategies converge, competition usually hovers around incremental improvements of quality, price, or both.

Trendsetters with wandering eyes are not content to stay fenced in by their industry's traditional walls. They prefer to stray to unfamiliar turf, busting through conventional boundaries that define an industry. Operating with wandering eyes usually comes in two forms:

- Defining a value offering that is superior to what two or more other industries provide.
- Gleaning ideas from other countries or adapting methods from other industries.

Venture Law Group (VLG), for example, redefined what a law firm could do for entrepreneurial startups. Founder Craig Johnson focused on serving startups that had great ideas but no cash to spend on exorbitant legal fees. These startup entrepreneurs were stymied by incomplete services among a group of industries: Venture capitalists got them funding. Management consultants offered business advice. Executive recruiters assembled top talent. And finally, law firms handled the barrage of legal transactions. Startup entrepreneurs were forced to deal with a variety of substitute industries without a one-stop shop, integrated service approach—until VLG came along.

Aptly located in Silicon Valley, VLG initially resembled a venture capital firm. Because of its great track record for discovering startups that had the best probability of success, VLG commanded credibility among venture capitalists and the entrepreneurial community. After selecting a promising entrepreneurial vision, VLG spent weeks on a business plan and financing strategy at no cost to the client until financing was arranged. Once a deal was conceived, VLG required a small equity position in the new company.

In addition to possibly scoring a financial windfall, VLG gained a powerful position in its customer's mind—as full-fledged business partners rather than easily replaced legal advisors. Only after the investors' financial package was assembled did traditional legal services and hourly billings commence.

In an entrepreneurial startup niche, VLG appears to have all the value bases covered. Instead of competing against law firms, they have invented a one-stop shopping destination for entrepreneurs with bold ideas.

How to get your eyes to wander

- Write a list of companies of which you are a raving fan. For each company on the list, write down the specific practice that you love. Then imagine how each practice could be adapted to your industry.
- Examine the hassles other industries are implicitly asking their customers to accept. What solutions could you bring to bear regarding these unmet customer needs? A prime example is Microsoft's ability to provide electronic solutions to the latent needs of a wide variety of industries. Microsoft Expedia outpaces the websites the travel industry has put together. Car Point Software provides detailed comparisons between automobile makes and models, offers the dealer price, allows a buyer to survey a variety of auto insurance policies, and to apply on line. Even online checking and newspaper advertising are available using Microsoft products. As David Kirkpatrick of *Fortune* says, "Watching Microsoft encroach on your industry is like seeing an elephant

head for your rose garden." If solving the hassles of other industry's customers works so spectacularly for Microsoft, why not you?

- Apply metaphors and analogies to reconceive your company and its products and services. National Basketball Association Commissioner David Stern unabashedly admitted to modeling his league's branding strategy after Disney and McDonald's. In the 1990's, faced with a mature filling-seats-in-the-arena business (arenas were nearly filled to capacity for the average game), Stern reconceived the NBA as a full-fledged entertainment business. NBA players are seen as individual superstars headlined in promotions even ahead of their teams. In the same way that Disney has Mickey Mouse and Donald Duck, the NBA has had characters such as Charles Barkley and Dennis Rodman. While Disney and McDonalds appealed to youth as prime customers, the NBA forged relationships through stay in school and drug prevention programs, as well as *Inside Stuff*, a youth-oriented TV show. Just as Disney is much more than a theme park, the NBA diversified its product line beyond ticket revenues to include apparel, logo licensing, videotapes, digital game broadcasts (*NBA.com*), and basketball trading cards.

- Alter your perspective by taking trips to foreign countries, or by developing relationships with international members in your trade association.

- Trace the initial and follow-up activities associated with the use of your product or service. Put yourself in the consumer's shoes and envision what happens before, during, and after your product is used. What other vendors do your consumers currently reach out to for services? Which services might your business provide to gain a greater share of profit? If it is not feasible for your business to offer the service, what partnerships and alliances could furnish the services in a referral or cross-selling model?

Imagining Eyes Create Hindsight in Advance

Replicators and trendsetters observe the future from very distinct vantage points. To use a sports analogy, replicators get to be Monday morning quarterbacks critiquing the actions of the active players. Waiting for changing circumstances to shake out, they watch the interaction of their competitors' moves and emerging trends before executing their own strategic responses. But as observers on the sideline, they live in constant fear that the whistle will blow to end the game before they set foot on the field of play. Replicators run the risk that the window of opportunity to capitalize on an evolving trend will shut down before they can act.

Creating hindsight in advance amounts to giving up the false sense of safety on the sidelines and stepping onto the field with both feet while the rules of the game are in flux. The trendsetters pre-game scouting report about the future consist of two primary elements: 1) experts' assumptions about trends likely to effect the far future; and 2) actual observations of changes that are already happening but haven't yet emerged as full-blown trends. Using this information, trendsetters discern trends that are likely to have decisive impact on their industry, and then imagine what latent needs would intensify if the trend plays out to its logical conclusion.

Kinkos is a good example of a company that capitalized on several emerging trends. Originally established in the 1970s to provide copy services on college campuses, Kinko's now serves an entirely different clientele—business people. Its transformation began in the 1980s, when CEO Paul Orafela and his team noticed several emergent trends—layoffs, outsourcing office functions, and the home office boom.

Kinko's soon became the world's leading provider of document solutions and business services. In addition to copies of all kinds, Kinko's offers 24-hour access to color printing, finishing and presentation services, Internet access, videoconferencing, and Web-based printing and document management. They have formed strategic alliances to expand offerings to both business and personal needs. For example, Kinko's and Fed Ex provide customers with late drop-off locations around the world.

Kinko's dramatic migration to the business marketplace illustrates strategic foresight based on noticing potential trends and then imagining the needs that would be evident once the trend fully took hold. Kinko's top competitors, including Sir Speedy and Pip Printing, probably had the same trend information, but lacked Kinko's imagining eyes.

How to create hindsight in advance

Organize a trend-clipping service within your own company. Encourage departmental teams to scan the periodicals they normally read and clip out any articles about trends that might affect your business. Assemble the trend information in files and circulate them among team members. At a monthly meeting, select the highest rated trends and ask questions like: How would the world look if any single trend or cluster of trends gained full expression? What needs would intensify among your customers and your customers' customers? How can we gain further insight into this trend and influence its direction and speed?

Imagine a team focused on the following set of trends:

- **Trend:** In the United States between 2000-2010, the 55-64 year old population will grow 74 percent, and the 65+ group will grow 54 percent. These are the only two groups anticipating growths in the double-digits.
- **Trend:** In the next 10 to 20 years, the huge population of Baby Boomers will be retiring.
- **Trend:** The Baby Boomers will not be aging gracefully, nor will they accept the limitations of aging. Witness the growing number of weekend athletes. Their participation is increased by the revolution in sports equipment to compensate for declining physical capacity, such as the oversized Prince tennis racquets, designed to make it still possible to execute hard-to-reach volley returns. The popularity of Viagra is a clear expression of the desire to stay young.
- **Trend:** At the time they retire, Baby Boomers will have the greatest wealth and discretionary income of any generation.

- **Trend:** A large segment of these retirees will not have children to care for them, either because of geographic distances, or the choice to remain childless.

With those five pieces of information in mind, the potential services for Boomer retirees are abundant in a variety of industries. For the construction industry, more seniors will want to live at home for as long as possible and avoid institutional care, so remodeling or building new homes with physical limitations in mind is a potential growth opportunity. What about a senior concierge service targeted for affluent retirement havens whose residents refuse to be limited by what Medicare will reimburse, but can't afford live-in caregivers? This service would provide the assistance generally given by children, such as physician referrals and healthcare advocacy, paying bills, housekeeping, providing personal chefs to prepare meals, running errands, and arranging transportation. Consider a networking service for seniors to connect with peers with like interests and hobbies, travel companions, or even romantic relationships. What about the plight of RV retirees who prefer to spend their time accessing the Internet for emails, travel information, and stock prices? In remote areas such as a KOA campsite in Montana, where the cable pickup looks like snow and there's not a Blockbuster within 200 miles, high-tech companies could offer Internet-based TV and movies. Finally, could you fathom a consulting service that advises existing businesses on new opportunities to extend their core competencies or reformat their retail outlets to serve seniors?

Belonging Eyes Produce a Network of Relationships

Is it possible that customers could become loyal fans because they bond with each other in a sense of shared affiliation with what a company stands for? We are witnessing a changing sense of affiliation in our society that substitutes particular social organizations for the traditional nuclear family. In their book *The 500 Year Delta*, Watts Wacker and Jim Taylor contend the new social organization comprises neo tribes, affinity groups, and fraternities of strangers.

If not among family members, where do people congregate? Think of the gregarious gang at the bar on *Cheers* or the male bonding that typifies 50,000-seat stadiums full of Promise Keepers. Think of Star Trek conventions thronged by costumed trekkies, and people spending hours "talking" in Internet chat rooms. Let's not forget extreme sports fanatics, physical fitness enthusiasts, self-improvement junkies, the Martha Stewart crowd, and environmental crusaders.

What if a company orchestrated the affiliation of its own customers who share a common love of the product or service? This points us in the direction of escaping the tired and drab marketing jargon of "demographics," into a perspective I call "belonging eyes," which acknowledges the latent need for bonding with other people who share similar values and interests. The unique opportunity comes when an affinity group sees a product, service, or company as its rallying point.

The hands-down innovation catalyst in capitalizing on the need for belonging is Harley Davidson. The motorcycle company's ingenious customer network, known as the Harley Owners Group, is a 15-year-old program with 325,000 members and 940 chapters that are closely connected by hobby and lifestyle. The company offers education for 7,000 chapter officers on how to attract new members, how to organize events, even whether to incorporate or not. Harley Davidson is far more than a motorcycle company to customers; it is the headquarters of the "open road" fraternity.

Growing a tribe of business revolutionaries

Less famous than Harley, but highly effective in tribalizing customers is *Fast Company* magazine. The *Fast Company* tribe is comprised of four groups who have a thirst for business transformation but lack a common platform for sharing their passion and challenges.

According to editor Alan Webber, "We cut across the boundaries of traditional magazines to a community that didn't know it was a community. In large companies, our readers are the influencing agents, early adopters of change, and restless souls. Their counterparts in 'young companies' are the top executives who seek to reinvent categories or change their industries. A third group is idea merchants and thought leaders who might come from areas like marketing, advertising, and management consulting. The final group is free agents and solo practitioners."

The magazine makes every effort to facilitate communication among its revolutionary brigade. E-mail addresses are lavishly spread in letters to the editor, "Community Pages," and at the end of each article. Two annual conferences encourage member networking and the chance to meet the revolution's heroes, who are speakers on the program.

On the website, the Company of Friends (COF), magazine readers in a local geographic area are linked into online discussion forums and chapter meetings. Each COF local chapter has a volunteer community coordinator who organizes local meetings and publishes minutes to update newcomers. Each community member can create a digital business card that describes personal activities, interests, and career vision.

According to Webber, "The Community of Friends just happened in a self-organizing way. We don't run it. We have enabled it. We were the medium." By the middle of 2001, 40,000 readers in 160 local areas were participating in COF.

How to gain the vantage point of belonging eyes

- View the collection of magazines at any newsstand to spot affinity groups that might comprise a portion of your target markets.
- Figure out a cause your company might champion. For example, besides selling boots and leather goods, Timberland mobilizes community action efforts by employees and customers.
- Think of an event your company could orchestrate that would draw your targeted affinity groups to participate.
- Select an affinity group that currently doesn't exist in an organized way but would find your products and services appealing. Based in Santa Barbara, California, The Innovation Network promotes conferences and information exchanges

between people in corporations, government, and universities who love innovation and may feel isolated within their own organization. The Million Dollar Round Table (MDRT) is a trade association that sets arbitrary standards of life insurance sales production to qualify for its elite membership status. Members receive education from the top sales people in the life insurance industry and a variety of motivational and personal growth experts. MDRT creates its own culture around the theme of the Whole Person Philosophy.

Wet Eyes and Dry Eyes: Combine Emotion and Function

Head-to-head competition often forces strategies into two polarized orientations. Some industries converge around the price and function of their products and services, with an appeal to rationality or "dry eyes." Other industries try to create a positive experience, with an appeal to emotionality or "wet eyes." And customers have gotten used to expecting these traditional orientations with particular industries.

From function to emotion: The supermarket as a tourist attraction

"For 40 years customers told our industry they were bored with shopping. They just wanted to get in and get out quick," said John Campbell, VP of HEB's Central Market Division. "In the early 1990s our top management began talking about a store whose mission was all about food and providing a distinctive shopping experience."

Supermarkets are one of the ultimate expressions of functional orientation. But the HEB team was asking intriguing questions. What if they designed a supermarket as an entertaining experience, where people looked forward to spending their leisure time? Then, instead of intruding on customers' busy schedules, shopping could be enjoyed and savored.

At the division's pilot store in Austin, Texas, HEB set out to transform shopping into an emotionally uplifting endeavor. Central Market's team of planners realized that a store could be distinctive for what it *didn't* sell as well as for what it did. They got rid of omnipresent consumer brands such as Budweiser, Tide, Frito-Lay, and Coke, and replaced them with a rich assortment of specialty foods. Their guiding principle: Don't blur uniqueness by trying to be all things to all people.

"When it came to merchandising, we drove a stake in the ground," Campbell said. "Everything had to taste good and couldn't be complicated to prepare. Our buyers only purchased the highest quality in natural, organic, or specialty foods. You could find a phenomenal produce or seafood department in separate specialty stores around Austin, but not under one roof, which was our objective."

It was one thing to make great products available but another to get people to change their diets, tastes, and shopping habits. In response to this challenge, Central Market created activities that were both entertaining and educational. A chef was hired to staff the cooking school. Customers paid $35 to shop the aisles for ingredients, while at the same time being educated about new products. They then returned to the kitchen to prepare an eight-course meal for 20.

Consumers who wanted to enjoy a night free from food preparation could dine on any of four distinct cuisines at the in-store restaurant, complete with inside seating or picnic tables on a wooden deck shaded by trees.

As for pure entertainment, Central Market hosted concerts two nights a week, including country, Big Band, blues, jazz, and rock music. Special Kid's Days offered parties, arts and crafts, and contests. The store also featured a massage station, a gift-wrapping station, and food-tasting nights.

The Austin Central Market regularly produces one million dollars in sales a week. HEB currently has plans for six stores in this format in major Texas cities. This original shopping experience makes Central Market the second most visited tourist attraction in Austin, behind the State Capital Building.

From emotion to function:
No-frills treatment for hernias

Industry executives tend to overrate the value customers place on the emotional experience associated with business transactions. For every guest that cherishes the friendly check-in and thorough facility orientation of a Ritz Carlton, there are others who would prefer the bellman to hand over the room key so they can head straight to their rooms.

Health care services are no exception. Going against the tide of upgrading customer service in health care, Shouldice Hospital in Thornhill, Canada, offers no private rooms, no phones or televisions in the rooms, no fresh sheets on the beds, and no room service for meals! In this spartan environment, they have achieved the distinction of operating with both the lowest costs and the best outcomes of all North American hospitals on one specific operation—hernias. There is simply no better place to go for high quality hernia surgery.

The Shouldice Method is based on the medical finding that early post-surgery movement speeds recovery. Patients usually walk out of the operating room and keep walking to the communal TV room and phone bank, to the cafeteria for group meals, and around the extensive hospital grounds. The average stay is only three days.

Besides having great surgeons, Shouldice is masterful at creating a healing culture among the staff and patients. Stressed-out new admissions are paired as roommates and in-dining table-mates with patients who have gone through the operation. Their newfound buddies share the experience of the procedure, offer reassurance, and above all, serve as living proof that everyone survives.

The patient interaction is so memorable that about 1,400 former patients return for the Shouldice Hospital Annual Reunion and Free Hernia Inspection.

While Shouldice Hospital counters the trend of many hospitals that provide more upscale services to stir positive emotions, its patients still gain emotional connection through their interactions with fellow patients, at no extra cost.

How to adjust the moisture in value offering

- Decide which value orientation has historically dominated your industry—emotionality or functionality. Now try the opposite orientation. Design your products and services and means of distribution to accentuate the opposing value orientation.

- If you emphasize emotionality, think of ways to raise the level of customer intimacy by securing unusual data like their hobbies, university affiliation, favorite sports, and preferences in music, reading, and the arts. How can you use this customized information to dazzle the customer?

- Imagine that Steven Spielberg was running your business. How would he design your customers' experience so they would be emotionally moved? Notice how the entertainment industries use all the senses—sound, taste, sight, touch, and smell—to orchestrate experiences.

- If you emphasize functionality, imagine that Michael Dell or your favorite high-tech visionary was in charge of your business operation. How might technology be used to give customers the basic service faster, with more convenience and lower cost?

- What if you had to run your business with a skeleton crew of people compared to today's number of employees? How could you deliver increased functional value by sharing work with customers in exchange for lower price or by using technology to streamline the process?

The Power of Fresh Eyes

We have had the phrase "knowledge is power" drilled into our heads in self-improvement tapes until it registers as truth. More accurately, knowledge discovered through fresh eyes is power. The trendsetter's formidable task is to observe what everyone is familiar with, but from an unusual vantage point, in order to conceive original customer insights and business opportunities.

The trendsetting perspective is less about being smart and more about being imaginative—developing the perspective no one else has about your products, services, and most important of all, customer needs. In the competitive game of innovation, original perspective is indispensable.

Chapter

6

The Power of Questions

Chapter

The Power of Questions

"The tragedy of adult life is that we are much more likely to fulfill our perceptions about how the world works than we are to fulfill our goals, ideals, and visions... We don't allow ourselves enough space for not knowing."

—Richard Pascale author of *Managing on the Edge*

Proven answers are less valuable than questions that have no answer. Questions stimulate a search for answers and plant ideas that nourish innovation.

By contrast, "knowing it all" stifles discovery. Replicators, who prefer to stay with the known, eliminate the prospect of conceiving anything boldly original by suppressing questions with versions of the statements, " I'm a veteran of this industry. I know how this business works."

What are the provocative questions that trendsetters use to devise their original strategies?

While replicators think they've got everything figured out, trendsetters want to find out what they don't know. They make a practice of raising provocative questions for which they have no answers. In fact, the primary goal isn't even coming up with answers, but in formulating the kind of questions that might reveal unforeseen possibilities, an advantage that will become more apparent as we examine Big Idea #5:

> **Big Idea #5: Questions are the seeds of innovation.**

Questions that produce penetrating customer insights and exceptional business opportunities don't appear out of thin air. To jumpstart your journey to assembling your own powerful set of strategic questions, I am going to give you the list that I have developed with my clients, called the Turock 29.

I didn't conceive the list of questions while sitting alone at my computer. The Turock 29 evolved over the past six years from several sources. As a management consultant, I've guided teams through a series of exercises to stimulate out-of-the-box thinking. In one exercise, I've asked them, "What are the questions you don't currently have answers for, but if you did have solid answers, would make a major difference in achieving your long-term vision?" Their responses were posted on a flip chart. After careful scrutiny, the most original questions made my master list. The current version of the Turock 29 contains input from groups as diverse as drywall tools salesmen and high tech business strategists.

A second source of questions was the actual innovators. With clients who had produced an innovative product, service, or business model, I routinely asked key contributors to tell me what questions they'd contemplated at the start of their work on the innovation.

Finally, I derived questions by reading books and magazine articles about business visionaries who described their actual innovation process. Sometimes they shared their exact questions. Other times, the questions could be inferred from how they explained their customer insights or interpretations of trend information.

Here's the latest version of the Turock 29 questions for developing strategic foresight, organized by key categories.

The Turock 29

Big picture issues

1. What accomplishment or result do you believe is extremely difficult or impossible to accomplish now, but if it could be done, would most powerfully increase your company's long-term profitability?

2. What is the issue you occasionally lose sleep over? What is the issue that is not urgent today, but if it goes unresolved, could ultimately jeopardize your long-term vision?

Operating assumptions

3. What is your company's winning formula? What assumptions are you making to explain your company's current success? What are the foreseeable circumstances where relying on these strategies could limit rather than enhance your future results?

4. What business are you really in? Not what your product catalogue suggests or where you are listed in the yellow pages, but what is the customer really buying? How can you stretch the " box" from which you define your business?

5. What are the conventional rules for success in your industry? If you broke the rules and did just the opposite, what opportunities might open up?

Collaborative opportunities

6. What opportunities could you develop through collaboration that would be impossible operating as an isolated business? Collaboration could involve a company's business units, strategic alliances and partnerships, or cooperation among members of a supply chain.

Customer value

7. What is a value offering, such as operations excellence, customization of service, or product innovation, that you could develop to such a level of superiority that you could practically "competitor-proof" your key accounts?

8. Five years from now, who will be your customers? How does your current product offering need to change to serve an aging customer base? How can you market, distribute, and

innovate your products to reach younger customers and gain their loyalty early on?

9. What are the classic customer frustrations you and your competition consider "the nature of the business" for which no one has come up with unique or cost-effective solutions? How can you design your customer contacts to remove every shred of aggravation?

10. What are the most pressing needs of your customers' customers? What solutions can you provide for these needs?

11. What are the new services your leading-edge customers are starting to request?

12. Based on your knowledge of future trends, what are the emerging customer problems that are likely to intensify in the future? Consider trends in demographics, technology, lifestyles, business, and legislation.

13. Think of your most profitable customers or market niche. If you didn't have their business, what would you be willing to do to get it?

14. What service would your customers ideally like to have, but would never request because they don't believe you can provide it?

15. As your customers downsize, what are the labor intensive activities and entire functions they might outsource? How might you address these new needs?

16. What blind spots do your customers fail to see in their strategy development? What are the threats to their vision that they don't notice? What are the budding opportunities they are also missing?

17. As industries undergo consolidation, what new problems confront both the large and small players respectively? Which problems can your business target to solve?

18. If all customary budget and human resource constraints were removed, what solutions can you dream up to resolve customer frustrations and compromises?

Organizational capacities

19. If you are to become the organization you envision in the future, what do you need to be doing today? What capabilities will you need to develop or acquire to equip yourself to serve future customers in ways they would never expect?

20. Consider core competencies that you are renowned for doing exceptionally well, such as total quality management, leadership training, consumer education, new product introduction, or supply chain management. Which competencies could be offered as value-added services to existing customers or even customers from other industries?

21. How can you develop your company culture so it becomes a source of competitive advantage? In what ways can your culture be used to increase customers' emotional connection to your brand?

Competition and other industries

22. Who will be your competitors in the future, not just today's recognized industry rivals but encroaching companies from other industries who can offer new value to your customers?

23. How competitively unique is your view of the future of your market? To stimulate original thinking, list the well-recognized future trends in your industry. Then go one step farther and speculate on the second- and third-order changes that might transpire and which may be off your competitor's radar screen. Given these ripple effects, what customer needs will become more pronounced?

24. What is the driving trend likely to effect your customers in the next five years? How can you capitalize on this trend better than your competition?

25. What companies outside your industry do you love doing business with? Which of their best practices do you value? How could those best practices be adapted to your business?

Reframing current realities

26. How might your business be reconfigured if its products and services were offered electronically?

27. If your dominant market were "mature," where would you go for new business opportunities?

28. If you were part of a new senior management group selected to replace incumbents just fired by the board of directors, what fresh ideas would you pursue?

29. If you set out to design your innovations to be hard for the competition to copy, what would you do? What actions would you take as far as a new business model, raising service standards through the roof, and rethinking roles so your employees offer unsurpassed value?

Questions as Seeds for Innovation

Although there is no way of predicting which of these 29 questions will be most productive to investigate for your business, I have selected three that consistently produce the greatest benefit for my clients. Let's examine their application to strategic issues in order to illustrate their power and effectiveness.

Define the nature of your business

Of all the questions on the Turock 29, the most important involves defining the nature of your business. This single question (Question 4) conditions everything a company is—the filter through which all other information passes. Therefore, it effects everything the company sees and determines eventual actions. The definition of the business is the ultimate screening criteria that signals managers which opportunities to pursue and which to reject as "not appropriate for our business." The business definition establishes the parameters for potential products, services, customers, competitors, and methods of going to market. Given the serious consequences, rethinking the basic business we are in should be done every few years. Yet in most cases, the original definition of the business was made in an implicit way, and over the years, very few established companies give this question a second thought.

Strategic planners can brainstorm a number of possible definitions of the nature of the business before settling on one. There are three basic criteria to use in defining a business: by the product you are selling, by the benefits that customers receive, and by the portfolio of core competencies. For example, McDonald's at different points in its history has defined itself as being in the:

- Hamburger business. Signs tabulated the number of hamburgers sold chain wide (product-based definition).
- Fast food business. The menu was broadened to include packaged salads, chicken, and breakfast items (product-based definition).
- Franchising business. McDonald's was one of the first franchise organizations to standardize operations to improve consistency of service globally (core competence definition).
- Commercial real estate business. The company's ability to spot prime store locations made its products easily accessible to customers (core competence definition).
- Youth entertainment business. Children's play areas, joint marketing with Disney, and serving Happy Meals illustrate McDonald's commitment to creating loyal customers while they are young (customer benefit definition).

McDonald's isn't alone in generating sales growth from business redefinition. The Chamberlain Group, the world's largest manufacturer of garage door openers, including the Liftmaster brand, has defined itself as the "home automation business." Consequently, its product line can be expanded to include automated gates, awnings, and just about anything where a motor can replace human labor.

Ukrop's Supermarkets, a chain in Richmond, Virginia, envisions being "a world class provider of services." This definition allows it to own a chain of in-store banks and a uniform business. Several of Ukrop's pharmacies offer wellness programs and disease management services for asthma, diabetes, high blood pressure, and cholesterol.

Redefining your business doesn't guarantee you will discover a better competitive advantage. Should you define your business in a way that encourages diversification? Or is a more narrow-niche, specialist definition the better route to take? You can't be certain. The benefit in exploring a range of business definitions is to trigger imagination.

Here are three steps to follow in addressing this question of paramount importance:

- First, list as many possible business definitions. Use the three criteria to define your business according to its products, customer benefits, and its set of core competencies.

- Second, evaluate each definition in conjunction with the other elements of a strategic position defined in Chapter 2. Begin with the sentence stem, "If we define our business as X...." When trying on a particular business definition, you naturally explore the implications in determining your customers, competitors, products and services; methods of sales and distribution; core competencies to acquire; future trends to pay attention to; sources of competitive advantage, and so on.

- Finally, select one definition. How do you make the right call? The key is to find a definition that leverages your company's unique capabilities in comparison to your competitors. Find a definition of your business that features your strengths (those existing and those to be developed) as they relate to a particular customer segment in a way that your competition will have a tough time matching. This step also requires understanding how your key competitors' decisions reflect their business definitions.

The business definitions of trendsetting companies share one thing. They are all original definitions that permit breaking the established rules of competition. In stark contrast to the stodgy financial services firms, Charles Schwab defines itself as a "maverick retailer." How can a services firm, with no inventory to sell, call itself a retailer? In an interview for the *Arthur Anderson Retailing Issues Letter,* President and CEO David Pottruck says, "Retailing is not an activity. It's a state of mind. Retailing is a much livelier, more exciting horse to ride than the carousel pony of financial services. Like the best retailers, we are concerned about the customer experience." This unique mindset, originating from Schwab's business definition, promotes constant industry-leading innovation, thought to be radical at the time they were introduced. Schwab was first to create discount brokering, while full-service brokers cringed at the prospect of losing fat commissions by letting customers make their own stock-buying decisions. In 1982, Schwab was first to introduce 24-hour, seven-day-a-week order entry and quotes. Another revolutionary move was developing a one-stop shop for mutual funds known as OneSource, which did away with charging clients for the convenience of buying all their mutual funds in one place. Finally, Schwab made the high stakes decision to cut trade commission fees in half when it became an online brokerage. In the first quarter of 2000, 73 percent of Schwab's total trading volume was done from Web-based trades.

Could Schwab have accomplished these trendsetting strategic moves if it defined itself as a traditional brokerage? Unlikely. The traditional brokerage business model is built on commission fees as a major source of income. Adopting the identity of a maverick retailer gives Schwab the perspective needed to dare to break the rules and to consistently do what's best in the interest of their customers.

Envision ideal services

Question 14 shakes up any preconceived notion of industry service levels. It asks, "What is the ideal service customers would like to have but never would request, thinking, 'I know it's not possible but...?'" This question has been responsible for launching a large number of sales growth surges.

An example is Progressive Insurance, which breaks all the rules in the auto insurance industry. Instead of processing paperwork on accident claims, they treat accidents like emergencies. Immediate Response is Progressive's 24-hours-a-day, ultra-fast claims service. Would you believe the company dispatches mobile units to accident scenes where the adjuster determines repair costs on a laptop and often issues a check on the spot? The industry measures claims settlement time in days; Progressive measures it in hours.

Progressive's incredible response time creates a huge competitive advantage. First, speed lowers costs. By completing damage inspections quickly, repairs get done sooner and Progressive pays fewer storage lot and rental car fees. Claims reps get most of their work done in the field, so fewer reps are needed. And on-site inspection curbs fraudulent repair claims by body shops or fake injuries. Ultimately, lower costs allow Progressive to specialize in a niche where competitors can't afford to go—the non-standard or high-risk driver.

But Progressive doesn't stop there. They came up with an insurance rate comparison service, known as Express Quote. As Willy Graves, General manager of Progressive's Great Plains Agency describes, "We want to make it easier for customers to shop for auto insurance. We tell anyone shopping for insurance our price for coverage and the comparable price for the three largest insurance companies in their state. We want all auto insurance customers to call us. When they grasp what we're doing, customers are surprised by this generous sharing of information."

Besides exceeding customer expectations at the risk of losing business, what's in it for Progressive? Being a central clearinghouse of insurance information results in the acquisition of sales leads. Every time quotes are shared, Progressive gets the caller's name, address, policy expiration date, and the payment rate with Allstate, State Farm, or whomever is the current low price insurer. This database gives Progressive the opportunity to initiate contact when they have a new program or superior rates.

Initially, Express Quote was piloted in California with a $20 charge. Nobody called for quotes. The traditional insurer sees a service that is losing money and discontinues it. As contrarians, Progressive saw the possibility of developing a massive prospect database and decided to do it for free. Express Quote began in 1993, long before price comparison was available on the Internet.

Progressive's strategists broke the rules when they dreamed up these ideal services. And then provided it, even though everyone then and now might say this level of service is impossible.

Add value through technology

With all the hype that the Internet will change the world as we know it, why does Question 26, "How might your business be reconfigured so its products and services are offered electronically?" even make the Turock 29? Here is the sad news. Replicators have captured the Internet. Rather than stretching the limits of amazing new services, the emphasis has been on efficiencies. So we are left with streamlined procurement, better order tracking, automated tech support, and leaner inventories. Are you impressed?

Now let's push the envelope to a radical Internet approach—cyber cemeteries. Prior to a keynote speech to the International Cemetery and Funeral Association, I interviewed several industry leaders about the trends likely to affect the death services industry. They were concerned because the number of cremations was rising, and more families were opting to forgo elaborate caskets and funeral services in favor of inexpensive urns. If this trend continued, the morticians would have to devise sales-generating services in addition to memorial events.

One such service that is slowly emerging is the "cyber cemetery." It involves developing a web site for the deceased containing materials prepared years before the person's passing. With the increased use of video camcorders, most families have plenty of footage to be spliced into a videotape. At the funeral home's video production studio, the director can assist clients in preparing a message to surviving family members.

The cyber-cemetery helps family and friends who cannot travel cross-country to visit a gravesite or who wish to stay connected with the deceased, especially during the grieving period. This system also preserves memories of a parent or grandparent for the next generation.

General Motors OnStar system uses a computer chip attached to the car's rear-view mirror to provide a dazzling array of value-added services.

By pressing the OnStar button, motorists are connected with a 24-hour concierge and emergency service. They can safely browse the Internet with their voices from the driver's seat, and have e-mails, stock quotes, and sports scores read to them. If the car's airbags deploy, OnStar receives a signal and calls to check the situation. In an accident, Advisors can contact the driver's insurance company, family members, the police, and emergency services. OnStar MED-NET ensures personal medical history, physician's name, current medications, and allergies are reported to hospital personnel.

Ever lock your keys in your vehicle? Tell your Advisor the PIN number, and a signal is activated to unlock the door. Lost your car in an airport parking lot? Call from your cell phone, and OnStar with automatically sound the car's horn and flash its lights.

What reconfiguring of services can be done in your industry? It is time for a trendsetter with fresh eyes to bring intriguing customer insights to the technology whizzes who can execute them.

No Time to Innovate

Most organizations realize the value of innovation, yet, so often I hear senior managers protest, "Where do we find the time to innovate? We all have our day jobs." The shareholders of publicly held companies won't stand for a couple of dismal quarters while senior management goes off to contemplate future innovations. Consequently, most business people are boxed into time frames for delivering results in the most expedient way possible. So strategizing for the future gets bracketed into a once-a-year strategic planning ritual. Expediency triumphs over innovation.

Here are four time-efficient practices my clients use to integrate the Turock 29 into a regular sequence of strategic conversations that occur throughout the year:

Weed out irrelevant questions. Be careful. Questions that first appear to be irrelevant to your business may be the most productive simply because you and your competitors have never asked them before.

Use the list to stimulate additional questions germane to your specific business issues. The Turock 29 is an excellent prototype, which any company can use to generate its own original questions.

Set regular meeting times to study select questions from your customized list. Every two to three weeks, spend an entire afternoon in a team meeting to create answers to pre-selected questions from your customized list. Assign the question(s) in advance, so team members can do preliminary research by interviewing suppliers and customers, searching the Internet, or consulting industry experts and trade magazines.

One caution: The first few meetings must produce compelling value otherwise this practice will be seen as a waste of time and fizzle out. When the first meeting is stimulating, you can expect team members to say, "We should do this type of meeting more often." When the value is clear, they are willing to find the time to prepare for the future.

Before you think that four hours every two to three weeks is a major expenditure of time, consider the routine used by one of my innovation-driven clients, a Fortune 100 consumer products manufacturer. The account team for a regional chain of a major national account spent Wednesday of every week engaged entirely in activities aimed at long-term issues. All conversations with customers had to lay the groundwork for future strategic moves, instead of the week's crises. The account team learned and applied out-of-the-box thinking techniques to hone their abilities to spot latent needs and develop innovative solutions.

One entire day each week amounts to 20 percent of the sales teams job, which seems like an extraordinary amount in a job where the singular focus is usually on delivering today's sales figures. Focusing on the future paid off for the account team's manager, who was soon promoted to a sales strategist position at the company's headquarters.

Apply the questions to field trips or other special assignments. One of my most innovative clients, a consumer products company, takes his sales team on field trips to experience other industries' customer service practices. Typically, they travel to a small town and spend a morning sampling the service of local business establishments. Beforehand, the team selects questions from the Turock 29 to discuss during their site visit. For example, his team might translate the questions into learning tasks like: Notice compromises that you witness customers tolerating; or make yourself an unofficial CIC (Chief Innovation Catalyst) and dream up ideal services that these businesses could attempt.

Conceive Your Own Original Questions

The human brain isn't built to churn out truly original questions on command. While provocative questions might emerge at any moment, certain practices increase your chances. Experiment with the following approaches to develop your own list of high impact questions.

- Maintain a file of innovative customer service ideas from different industries. For each idea, identify the latent need being addressed. Try to guess the questions that might have produced these innovations.

- Find out what questions your most progressive customers, supply channel partners, or trade association members were contemplating when they conceived their best innovations.

- Look at "new" industries and services (wellness, total quality in the 1960s, today's web and e-businesses) or professions (sports agents, executive coaches, dating services) that didn't exist decades back. What potential questions might the inventors of these services have been investigating?

- As you read business magazines and books, become an avid collector of questions. Instead of reading to retain information, concentrate on generating provocative questions. Notice questions in the text that are useful in their current form or with minor revision. In addition, be alert to any intriguing questions that occur as you read. Write them down in the book's margins or on a note pad.

The Leader as Master Questioner

In trendsetting companies, the model of "leader as master questioner" is more highly valued than "leader as answer man or woman." The best a leader can do is set the organization in the right direction and then create an environment where the interplay of team learning produces new answers to test against changing marketplace realities. Asking challenging questions is an excellent starting point.

Chapters 4-6 shared a common theme—focus on latent customer needs. We looked at the sources of latent needs, as well as "fresh-eyes" perspectives and provocative questions for spotting them. This trio of chapters offered a detailed glimpse at the extraordinary quality of thinking many business visionaries possess.

But the real make-or-break factor in innovation lies with a company's leadership team. Learning dozens of out-of-the-box thinking methods will be useless without leaders with the courage to stick their necks out in support of bold innovation. And it does require courage to place innovations that may not pay off for years to come at the top of your agenda, while Wall Street is screaming for impressive results this quarter. Trendsetting leaders are fearless in the face of any and all threats to innovation.

Chapter

7

Fearlessness Breeds Freedom

Chapter

7

Fearlessness Breeds Freedom

"Nothing splendid has ever been achieved except by those who dared believe that something inside them was superior to circumstances."

—Bruce Barton

If you aspire to be the only one to do what you do, you must be ready to take the strategic road less traveled. And if you hope to get your organization moving in the trendsetter direction, you, as a leader, must have the ability to think with the fearless freedom of an innovator.

The biggest hurdle for most organizations is that their leaders think like replicators. In facilitating a panel discussion of community leaders, I asked a bank president to describe the biggest obstacle stopping his company from conceiving an innovative strategy. "I'm the problem," he blurted out. "I don't have the imagination to appreciate my people's imagination."

What are the core beliefs that distinguish trend-setting leaders?

Most replicator managers would not have perceived their responsibility so clearly, or expressed it so willingly. This bank president was stuck, so his company remained stuck. The company couldn't go any farther than its leader could bring it—which brings us to Big Idea #6:

> **Big Idea #6: An organization's trendsetting capacity reflects its leadership beliefs.**

Understanding fear intimately

The scope of every organization's vision is linked to, and limited by, the leadership team's courage to conceive and execute an original idea, even one that appears to require unreasonable effort. The leaders' appetite for originality and achievement creates the ripple effect of freeing employees to be fearless in embracing the real, not illusionary, risks in undertaking a bold vision.

The bank president may have been extraordinarily honest, but he is not the only one afraid of innovation. The journey to becoming a trendsetter triggers fears. How will you remain calm and focus on results when the outcome of any innovation is so uncertain? How will you muster the conviction to stake out what appear to be unreasonable goals? Can you depend on your people to deliver a performance that exceeds anything they have previously done? An organization's trendsetting capacity is closely related to how well its leaders hold beliefs that diminish fear.

Few individuals were more certain of the connection between the leader's inner sense of freedom and the organization's capacity for bold action than Mohandas Gandhi, who wrote:

> *"The outward or political freedom we shall attain will be in exact proportion to the inward or spiritual freedom that we may have grown to as a result of our personal search. If this is the correct view of freedom, as I believe it is, then our energy must be focused on achieving revolution from within or freedom from fear."*

Gandhi believed it was the role of a leader to help followers free themselves from inner fear. "Fearless" doesn't mean ignoring the presence of fear or pretending it doesn't exist. Fearlessness begins with the courage to inquire into the source of fear, to understand it intimately. Getting to the bottom of fears reveals that many of them are rooted in imaginary catastrophes. They are illusions. Once people recognize the illusion, they are free to make a full range of choices. *Fear breeds phantom obstacles. Truth breeds fearlessness. Fearlessness breeds freedom.*

The freedom of trendsetting leaders is reflected in their thinking, which is considered so extreme that their industry's old guard would brand them as crazy. Notice the potential symptoms of this "craziness" in the following quotes:

> *"I want Sun to be controversial; if everybody believes in your strategy, you have zero chance of profit."*
> —Scott McNeally, CEO of Sun Microsystems

> *"You can't behave in a calm rational manner. You've got to be out there on the lunatic fringe."*
> —Jack Welch, CEO of General Electric who despite inheriting a crown jewel of a company in 1979, staged a series of revolutions during his tenure.

> *"You've got to have the mavericks in Cisco. You've got to have people who challenge you. It's like wild ducks. I don't mind wild ducks. I don't expect us to fly in formation. I just want us to go kind of south at the same time of the year, and when it's time to go north, to go north at the same time of the year."*
> —John Chambers, CEO, Cisco, in response to the question, "Would you hire Dennis Rodman?"

> *"A recession is coming in the airline industry again. That's the time to invest, to improve quality. So right now, we're ripping out everything inside and outside our planes and putting in double beds, single beds, beautiful baths, special masseuse and manicure areas. A lot of airline bosses take the opposite approach in a recession."*
> —Richard Branson, founder of Virgin Atlantic Airlines on future plans.

•••

Welcome to the charter membership of the business world's lunatic fringe. If you don't know the rest of their stories, you might think you're listening to certified crazies. But they repeatedly back up the unconventional verbiage with strategic moves that bring replicators to conclude, "Let's not go there."

The Freedom to Embrace Uncertainty

One erroneous belief held by replicator managers automatically constrains their freedom of choice. The belief is that *life is supposed to turn out according to plan.*

Closer scrutiny reveals that this belief is irrational. Plans don't always materialize. Nevertheless, replicator managers adopt a white-knuckle grip on the winning formula that brought prior success, no matter how much the business world around them changes.

Replicator managers' first impulse is to try to bring business operations to a point of stability, predictability, and reliability. They seek to be in control, and run a smooth, variance-free operation. When circumstances change dramatically so that old answers no longer work, then a sense of powerlessness takes hold.

To ward off this stress, replicators accept a dangerous tradeoff. In exchange for the false sense of security that comes with replicating the past, they sacrifice their ability to seize unexpected opportunities. Unknowingly, they place an invisible lid on their entire organization's aspirations. Success will always be incremental. But so will failure. Replicator strategies may not cause a company to crash and burn, but they will probably bring about its slow death.

Slow death is an unnecessary compromise. Instead, replace the illusion of being able to control how plans unfold with an empowering belief: *Life is a surprise.* This belief reveals the illusion in perceiving uncertainty as loss of a seemingly secure future. The belief also invites an empowering choice: You can see uncertainty as freedom to create a future that wasn't ordinarily going to happen.

Trendsetting leaders fully embrace the inevitable uncertainty of life, realizing that the business world is no exception. The expectation that life unfolds as a surprise has a profoundly freeing effect. Trendsetters can enjoy the marvelous trio of freedoms that come from a willingness to embrace uncertainty: creativity, learning, and security within oneself. Let's examine each one.

The first freedom is the increased opportunity for creative thinking that multiplies in uncertain times. Following rules, conventions, and established procedures increasingly fails to produce intended results. In contrast, the appearance of uncertainty provokes a search for original solutions and greater willingness to entertain previously unfathomable ideas. For trendsetting leaders, uncertainty is a creative opportunity to be exploited to the fullest. As the Roman poet Horace once said, "Uncertainty reveals genius; security conceals it."

A second freedom is an accelerated learning curve. Longshoreman and philosopher Eric Hoffer captured this shift of priorities when he asserted, "In times of drastic change, it is the learners who inherit the future; the learned usually find themselves equipped to live in a world that no longer exists."

The world is unlikely to return to the days when it was normal for someone to occupy the same job for years without drastically changing the required skills. Instead, workers will need to master new technologies and reinvent roles to accommodate an accelerated pace of change. Embarking on steep learning curves is the norm rather than the exception. The most valuable performers in 21st century business will be the fastest learners.

The third freedom is an enlarged sense of personal security. Contrary to popular opinion, real security is not based on how circumstances appear. Real security is founded on the inner confidence of knowing deep down that you and your team can handle any and all challenges.

Trendsetters' confidence is built on a staunch willingness to encounter the risks in doing something original, where the outcome is uncertain. With each fear acted upon, trendsetters keep expanding the range of circumstances they feel secure in facing. Healthy disregard for the unreasonable becomes their modus operandi.

Self-scrutinizing questions

To personalize the new sources of freedom that become available through embracing uncertainty consider the following questions.

1. Identify a bold strategic move you've been considering. If you choose to make the move, what new situations might you expect to face that will require you to grow as a leader?
2. What fears would you have the opportunity to master, thereby enlarging your capacity for risk-taking?
3. In what ways do your efforts to hold things together actually rob you of freedom to experiment, imagine, risk, and swing out boldly?

The Freedom to Declare a Desired Future

Trendsetting leaders set goals that often seem far-fetched. Being responsive to customer requests isn't good enough; anticipating what customers will want before they even know for themselves is the performance standard. When industry pundits agree that a strategy is certain to fail, trendsetters believe that judgment means they are on to something big.

How can trendsetters be so bold in their aspirations when there is no evidence their organization can produce the results they claim will happen?

The answer: They are not afraid to declare their vision of the desired future before the entire world.

I first learned about declarations in seminars developed by Landmark Education Corporation and later in the writing of Tracy Goss (*The Last Word on Power*) who stated: "A declaration is an act of speaking that brings forth a future the moment it is spoken."

Declarations convey a sense of urgency. Rather than getting ready to embark on a desired future *someday*, the declaration provokes action *right now* in a way that is consistent with bringing that future into reality. The declaration becomes a lingering reference that inspires both the leader and his or her followers to a person-on-a-mission focus on results.

From the moment the staff of Pike Street Fish Market in Seattle declared it would become "world famous," they began to scrutinize every aspect of their performance, wondering, "Will this contribute to our becoming world famous?"

For example, the "flying fish show," where workers hurl sockeye salmon across the crowds to the wrapping station, is so extraordinary that it has been featured on the *CBS Morning News* and in the best-selling corporate training video, "FISH!" made by ChartHouse International Learning Corporation. Fish monger John Yokoyama and his team are hired by huge corporations to consult on customer service and inspiring work environments. Could they have attained this level of fame without fearlessly declaring their ideal future?

When athletic director Ted Leland declared that Stanford University would have "the most dominant athletic program in the history of college athletics," he wasn't blowing smoke. At first, Stanford's coaches thought Leland's declaration was outlandish. But the announcement immediately led to reinventing fund raising efforts, investment decisions, recruiting objectives, and constructing facilities essential for delivering on the goal of athletic program dominance.

Nine years later, Stanford had won six consecutive Sears Directors' Cups, which are awarded annually to the nation's top athletic programs. Thirty-four Stanford athletes and coaches participated at the 2000 Olympic Games.

Starbucks has declared it will become "a great enduring company with the most recognized and respected brand in the world, known for inspiring and nurturing the human spirit." To make that declaration happen, the company does extensive consumer research in selecting business partners with the aim of preserving brand integrity. It has also embarked on global expansion and introduced branded products. To create a great place to work, Starbucks spends more money on training its 35,000 employees (partners) than in advertising, and offers stock options to part-timers.

What are the basic elements of the stand a leader must adopt for declaring a preferred future? First, the leader must be prepared to do whatever it takes to achieve the desired outcome, in spite of uncertainty about whether it can be done or how it should be accomplished.

Second, the leader must declare a desired future and take action despite the absence of agreement among team members and in the face of their disbelief, fear, and anger. These emotions are treated as a "positive crisis" and a welcome signal that the vision is sufficiently challenging.

Third, the leader makes declarations that defy expectations of what is possible based on past performance. The declaration is rooted in the understanding that repeating old solutions will not deliver on the current stretch goals. It forces people to find new means for achieving them.

Self-scrutinizing questions

1. What would you be committed to accomplishing, if only it were possible? Would you be willing to give up the security that following past precedents provides in order to pursue this commitment that seems impossible?

2. What are three or four declarations you could start today that might appear to be impossible projects? For instance, consider meeting impossible deadlines, setting a record for productivity in accomplishing a specific task, or handling a long-standing conflict in teamwork.

3. What kind of leader would you need to be to deliver the future you envision? Describe shifts in priorities, changes in how you appropriate time, and alterations in your style of producing results through people and teams.

The Freedom to Embolden Others

Before you read on, take this quiz. Which of the following statements do you believe to be true? No hedging. Pick one.

- *Statement 1:* The best measure of employees' capabilities is to look at their past results.

- *Statement 2:* The upper limit of employee performance is determined by the leader's belief in their capacity to give a great performance.

Statement 1 is unquestionably the most likely to be picked. Among replicator managers, this one would win by a landslide. Statement 1 supported a number of observations made by most managers. For example, after several months on the job, employees usually settle into a steady baseline level of performance. Any spurts of unprecedented positive results are attributed to lucky breaks or favorable circumstances. All companies have their share of superstars, average performers, and laggards. Lame ducks don't transform one day to soar amongst eagles. Outside of full responsibility for hiring decisions, managers are substantially stuck with the mixture of good and bad talent they have picked.

Statement 2 rests on what might sound like a preposterous notion— that employees have the capacity to give an unpredictably brilliant performance, and the chance of such breakthroughs occurring is linked to the level of performance their leader deems achievable. To take this notion one step further and make it more palatable requires seeing the connection between the leader's beliefs and ensuing actions. What a leader believes about employees' capacity for accomplishment determines the culture, incentives, organizational structure, and even coaching style in the organization—all of which eventually will determine an upper limit on results.

Leaders can choose to expect the highest standards of peak performance, extraordinary effort, or mastery. Or they can expect lower standards, settling for good enough, okay, fine, ordinary, and predictable. The grave implication is that the business strategy evolves either as an accommodation to team members' past performance or as a stretch to redefine their performance capacities.

Perhaps the most notable management expert espousing the correlation between a manager's inner beliefs and actual employee performance was Douglas McGregor, author of the book *The Professional Manager*, who said,

"The greatest disparity between objective reality and managerial perceptions of it is an underestimation of the potentialities of human beings for contributions to organizational effectiveness."

Not-so-great expectations

When replicator leaders believe people's potential is not likely to be significantly better than past history predicts, the following reactions ensue:

- Employees don't share valuable insights about customers that they glean from direct contact.
- Employees don't bother to rethink and improve work processes, perpetuating the motto: It's always been done this way.
- Employees don't exercise personal judgment for decisions, even when breaking the rules to satisfy a customer makes good business sense.
- Employees don't make an effort beyond their defined job description, contending, "It's not my job."

The unfortunate outcome of diminished expectations about employee performance is revealed in General Electric's experience when it first instituted Workout, an element of the company's own version of total quality management. Once Workout was in operation, GE managers were disturbed to discover the extent to which they had missed valuable input from their employees for many years. After completing the first-ever Workout session for his plant, one veteran GE Appliance worker shouted to his general manager, "For 25 years you've had my hands, when all that time you could have had my brain—for nothing."

Pre-Workout GE missed out on a sizeable share of its employees' discretionary energy. Discretionary energy is observable in people's curiosity, indomitable spirit, hunger for learning, willingness to stick their necks out in taking risks, seizing initiative for independent thinking, attention to detail, and passion for the product.

Tapping into the energy

How do trendsetting leaders tap into this discretionary energy? Here is where it gets tricky. You can pay people to put in their eight-to-five shift and do a decent day's work, but cash doesn't buy their discretionary energy. Discretionary energy is given voluntarily. It is a matter of personal choice. So the central leadership challenge involves creating an environment that actually unleashes people's freedom to choose to contribute their discretionary energy.

Eliciting discretionary energy starts with a leader's expectations of people. In my conversations with trendsetting leaders, their resolute faith in their people comes across in beliefs like:

- Work is as natural as play. People like or dislike it based on conditions that management can control.
- Under the right conditions, the average person will seek and accept responsibility rather than avoid it.
- Many people have the ingenuity and creativity needed to solve organizational problems. These qualities are not confined to a gifted few.
- Breakthroughs that defy past performance are possible at any moment.
- Work is an outlet for people's self-expression and a place where they can live their most passionate values.
- People have the capacity to be unstoppable in their pursuit of compelling visions.

One of the most dramatic examples of the impact of revamping performance expectations is depicted in the experience of CEO Ralph Stayer of Johnsonville Sausage. In an article in the *Harvard Business Review*, "How I Learned to Let My Workers Lead," Stayer explained his moment of insight into the limiting impact of his beliefs:

> *What worried me more than the competition, however, was the gap between potential and performance. Our people didn't seem to care...I had created a management style that kept people from assuming responsibility. Of course, it was counterproductive for me to own*

all the company's problems, but in 1980, every problem did, in fact, rest squarely on my shoulders, weighing me down and—though I didn't appreciate it at the time—crippling my subordinates and strangling the company. If I was going to fix what I had made, I would have to start by fixing myself. In many ways that was my good luck, or, to put the same thought another way, Thank God I was the problem so I could be the solution.

Ralph Stayer's "route-all-decisions-through-me" style of management crippled organizational learning and retarded his team members' intellectual capital. In taking accountability for the situation his leadership created, Stayer had to give up his belief, grounded in past experience, that "Anything I don't do myself will not be done right."

Pain is a great motivator. While Johnsonville's business had grown nicely, Stayer was unhappy with the business environment and realized that to improve results, he had no choice but to do what he feared most—trust employees to make decisions and even insist on being responsible for their piece of the business.

Stayer took on a new belief—"Those who implement a decision and live with its consequences, are the best people to make it." Adopting that belief ushered in fundamental changes. Top management stopped tasting sausage, and the people who made sausage started. If there was a problem with air leakage in the vacuum-packed plastic packages of sausage, a team of workers was responsible for working with suppliers to figure out a solution. Line workers responsible for correcting problems being raised answered customer complaint letters. When fellow workers gave sloppy or apathetic performance, the responsibility for correcting the problem rested with the shop workers. Senior managers consulted them in the writing of performance standards and in confronting poor performers. Ultimately, line workers earned the responsibility for hiring and firing their cohorts.

This flurry of changes led Johnsonville to becoming a pioneer in the 1990s movement toward self-managing teams. Self-managing extended to decisions about scheduling, budgeting, measuring quality, investing in capital improvements, and even making strategic decisions to take on major new accounts that would test manufacturing capabilities. Gradually, Johnsonville eliminated many management positions and developed a promotion system that rewarded building the problem-solving capabilities of other team members, rather than solving their problems for them.

Ralph Strayer's reinvention as a leader was captured in his new belief, "People want to be great. If they aren't, it's because management won't let them be." His courage to stop relying on his personal winning formula of being in control of all decisions and massively empowering employees is testimony to the notion—"fearlessness breeds freedom." By modifying systems and structures that grant employees the freedom to think for themselves, Stayer himself was freed up to invent an entire organization that is continuously learning.

Your employees' performance is a reflection of your expectations. If you believe that your employees' past performance is the best they can do, you won't see any value in dreaming up a bold strategy that requires more innovative thinking, faster learning, and wider decision-making responsibility. Your eventual strategy will need to compensate for your people's previously demonstrated level of performance capacity. In contrast, if you believe that employees are capable of doing great things, given the right organizational conditions, then your strategy will call for breakthroughs in performance.

Self-scrutinizing questions

Examine the following practices in your business to detect the underlying leadership beliefs about people's potential.

- *Hiring and training.* Are you looking for skills and experience or the right attitudes? Are there positions in your organization where you simply fill slots and expect aggressive turnover? What do your actions say about your expectations for your people?

- *Job descriptions.* How tightly are job descriptions followed and what tolerance is there to reinvent the job to bring greater value to internal or external customers? Are your jobs designed to make them as simple and routine as possible or is there room to gain customer insights and improve work processes?

- *Decision making.* What is the state of empowerment in your organization? What decisions do you trust people to make and how tightly do you adhere to protocol that reserves decisions for management? What is the dollar amount you would be willing to allow your employees to invest to solve a problem with no questions asked? What beliefs about faith in people's decision-making prowess are reflected in your practices?

- *Rewards.* What kinds of rewards are available? Are they reward contingencies weighted on the side of getting people to replicate the past in ways that are more, better, or slightly different? Are there rewards for coming up with innovative ideas and participating in new ventures even when they may not immediately produce favorable results?

- *Coaching and performance management.* What assumptions do you carry into coaching sessions with your average performers and how do they compare to those you bring to sessions with your star performers? How do you define your responsibility in producing results through others? Can you buy into the notion that your employees' results are a measure of your commitment to their excellence?

Gut Check

Trendsetting leaders exercise beliefs that are routinely designated as nonconformist, odd, or reckless by the orthodox establishment. When the top managers lead from a trendsetter belief system, their whole organization gains access to newfound power.

Perhaps the best quote for capturing the trendsetting leader's courage and freedom from inner fear was expressed by Gordon McKenzie, an innovation catalyst for many years at Hallmark, "To be nobody but yourself in a world which is doing its best night and day to make you like everybody else is to fight the hardest human battle anybody can fight and never stop fighting."

Chapter

8

The Spirit of the Garage

Chapter

8

The Spirit of the Garage

> *"History shows us that organizations achieve greatness*
> *when people are allowed to do unexpected things—*
> *to show initiative and creativity to step outside the scripted path."*
>
> —Dr. Jim Collins, management consultant

The founders of Apple Computer and Hewlett Packard started out in their garages and are among the many companies that spun out of Stanford University graduates into the Silicon Valley. Companies like these pioneered a way of doing business that attracted the creative energy I call the spirit of the garage.

In an article in the *Harvard Business Review* in 1967, Warren Bennis and Philip Slater pointed to "democratization of organizations" as an early sign of this trend. Democracy, they said, is the only system that effectively addresses the emerging conditions of contemporary civilization and businesses. In the Industrial Age, assembly-line efficiency was a strategy that met the needs of the era. In the Information Age, industry needs a fundamentally different business paradigm. As Bennis and Slater wrote, "democracy becomes a functional necessity whenever a social system is competing for survival under conditions of chronic change." The democracy these authors had in mind in the 1960s was a system of cultural values that included:

How do you develop a culture where strategic innovation flourishes?

- Free flowing communication.
- Reliance on consensus over coercion to manage conflict.
- Influential ideas given greater power over position in the chain of command.
- Rational mediation of the inevitable conflict between individual aspirations and organizational goals.

The spirit of the garage expresses the cumulative effects of these democratic trends. It is alive and well in pockets of entrepreneurial freedom that extend from Dell Computer in Austin, to Microsoft, Starbucks, and Amazon.com in Seattle. An excellent global expression of the spirit of the garage is Hong Kong, which offers conditions approximating entrepreneurial nirvana—no OSHA, no minimum wage, a flat 15 percent tax, and a one-day turnaround for approval of a business license. In the words of the Chief Executive for the Hong Kong SAR, Tung Chee-hwa in 1997, "The success of Hong Kong is the freedoms we enjoy. Freedom of every nature—freedom of thought, freedom of movement, freedom of the press, freedom of information, freedom to be creative."

In whatever industry or country that spirit-of-the-garage conditions occur, they create a hotbed of innovation where best-of-the-best and innovation catalyst strategies are the only games in town. In high tech industries, the edict, "differentiate or die" is a lightweight notion. "Be first or perish" is more accurate. The pursuit of latent needs is an eye-opening notion for ask-customers-what-they-want replicators, but rings synonymous with the Valley's universal mantra—"do something cool." In Silicon Valley, the funding source is not some number-crunching CFO who's idea of an erotic experience is to produce an impressive P&L, but venture capitalists who lust for sky's-the-limit opportunities even if they won't show profit for years ahead. In the Valley, a knowledge worker's concept of job security is not based on steady employment with one company, but having free reign to jump ship and relocate to the next cutting edge project.

Which brings us to the final crucial element in a trendsetting company—its culture. There is no sense in attempting to instill a trendsetting strategy in a culture that is designed for continuous improvement of traditional practices. In addition, cultures may be conducive to fresh ideas but still may be unable to carry out effective prototyping and new product introduction campaigns. Bankruptcy courts have dockets filled with lists of organizations whose inventions were brilliant but whose execution in the marketplace ruined cash flow. They lacked the effective organizational environment to sustain innovation, which brings us to Big Idea #7:

> **Big Idea #7: Develop a culture that aligns employee behavior with the organization's innovative strategy.**

The organizational culture dictates the team members' degree of entrepreneurial freedom. If you want cutting-edge innovation, create a culture that empowers people to exceed all normal expectations.

Organizational Disincentives to Innovation

If there is one value that typifies the spirit of the garage, it is devotion to bold ideas. To grasp the distinctiveness of this culture, let's examine how its opposite, a bureaucracy, handles efforts at innovation.

In a bureaucracy, future opportunities take a distant second place to sure bets in the short term. With this conservative bias implanted in the culture, the path from conception of an idea to linkage with appropriate resources becomes a tough-to-traverse obstacle course.

The first hurdle is a tacit restriction on who can contribute to the company's strategy. Bureaucracies almost never call for innovative ideas from the front line work force. Nor is their middle management likely to indulge in original thinking because being associated with a failed attempt at innovation could jeopardize future promotions. Only senior management is deemed to have the necessary big picture perspective for generating valuable strategic insights.

Bureaucratic organizations smother original ideas at lower levels in the company before they ever see the light of day. They burden the front line with short-term priorities, and a demand for what-have-you-done-for-me-lately results in sales, order processing, report writing, and customer service. News is floated about what happened to the infamous "last guy" who failed in an attempt at innovation, vividly recounting the negative consequences that he received for sticking his neck out and making a mistake.

New ideas in such organizations must run the gauntlet of due process procedures. Every potential innovator must:

- Provide reams of market research data to prove customer demand for the proposed innovation, even in the case of untested markets.
- Prepare an ironclad business case with guaranteed early return on investment.
- Make sure in advance that the idea doesn't threaten his/ her own department's talent pool or weaken its chances for delivering on objectives.

Should an innovation manage to survive all these hurdles, the sudden death rule appears: If one reviewer can't fathom the idea, it's history.

Now contemplate the devastating effects of this organizational environment on would-be innovators. Put entrepreneurial people through a funding approval process designed to reject any idea in the category of "We've never done anything like that before," and turnover soars. Reward the achievement of short-term goals, without acknowledging people for their efforts in mastering new competencies that support future innovations, and time allotted to professional development evaporates. Place idealistic knowledge workers in an organization saddled with a humdrum, long-term vision and prepare to receive half-hearted effort. Clearly a bureaucratic organizational environment does not align employee behavior with trendsetting strategies. That alignment comes from instituting the spirit of the garage.

The Five Cultural Values of a Trendsetting Organization

Let's use a variety of case examples to illustrate the spirit of the garage as it is expressed in the organizational culture. In this discussion, the "spirit" is summarized as the following core values:

1. Reverence for talent.
2. Inspirational missions.
3. Autonomy.
4. Nobility of mistakes.
5. Ad hoc innovation pockets.

Core value #1: Reverence for talent

"Talent wins championships," shouts the media announcer during a sporting event. "Great casting, writing, and directing win you an Oscar" is heard in Hollywood. The people in sports and the performing arts are well aware of the connection between high achievement and great talent. They have always known what businesses have to learn if they are to create a trendsetting environment. They understand that leaders who surround themselves with great talent look like geniuses.

Assembling talent begins with recruiting and hiring entrepreneurial individuals who can blend well with a trendsetting culture. In an article in *Fast Company*, Bill Birchard outlined three fundamental lessons for hiring top people that thrive in and contribute to innovative organizations.

To win the war for talent, hiring should involve everyone in the company. Finding great people is not just the domain of personnel or human resources. Yahoo's CEO Jeff Mallet said, "The people we hire should have their own short lists of great talent. Our own people's 'little black books' are our best form of recruiting." Cisco offers employees $1,000 whenever a referred applicant is hired, and CEO John Chambers tracks referral rates as a key performance indicator.

You must encourage talented creative people to find you. Great performers are not likely to read the help wanted ads so you need to build the buzz. Led by director of corporate employment, Michael McNeal, Cisco employed a number of unconventional-bordering-on-outrageous ways of attracting passive job seekers:

- The Cisco Web site let job candidates match their skills with job openings, and paired them with a volunteer "friend" in the organization who facilitated networking with the right people and offered guidance throughout the hiring process.
- At the 1997 Stanford-California football game, every time a team scored, a group of Cisco people seated in the end zones waved placards that spelled out *www.cisco.com/jobs.*
- Cisco had "sourcers" who studied trade press and searched through patent databases and conference proceedings to identify prestigious industry thought leaders.

Never settle for less. Realizing that rapidly adding thousands of new people would dilute the cultural attributes that had made the company successful, EMC of Hopkins, Massachusetts, a manufacturer of enterprise storage products, came up with a "success profile" that characterized great EMC employees. The profile featured seven categories: technical competence, goal-orientation, sense of urgency, accountability, external and internal customer responsiveness, cross-functional behavior, and integrity.

Self-scrutinizing questions

1. What are your hiring criteria, and who are you targeting—warm bodies, adequate workers, or peak performers?
2. Are you recruiting in ways that raise your odds of attracting top talent that fit with your culture?
3. How do talent-driven industries like sports and the performing arts go about recruiting and selecting top talent and how can you adapt some of their methods? Study practices like advance scouting, casting calls, auditioning, and their adaptation to your business.

Core value #2: Inspirational missions

Here is the quintessential recruitment story. When Steve Jobs was at a cocktail party in the heyday of Apple Computer, he said to John Scully, then the CEO of Pepsi, "John, how do you want to spend the rest of your career—selling sugared water or changing the world?" Read that question again. Jobs used the ideal screening question for a CEO who would fit into a culture where peak performance is inspired by the greatness of the company's mission.

David Packard, co-founder of Hewlett Packard, encapsulated this core value of a trendsetter during a speech given in 1960.

> *"I think many people assume, wrongly, that a company exists simply to make money. While this is an important result of a company's existence, we have to go deeper and find the real reasons for our being. As we investigate this, we inevitably come to the conclusion that a group of people get together and exist as an institution that we call a company so they are able to accomplish something collectively that they could not accomplish separately—they make a contribution to society, a phrase which sounds trite but is fundamental."*

Business consultant Roxanne Emmerich said the same in different words when she asserted, "Saying you are in business to make a profit is like saying you are alive to breathe." Profit is one of the vital signs that a company is alive. When profits are flat the game is over. But just like breathing is essential to sustain life, but is not the reason for life, profits are not the reason a company exists.

For example, when a Hewlett Packard engineer talks about getting a new product out the door, he doesn't think, "I put all my heart and soul into this project and worked outrageous hours because it will jack up our earnings per share by 25 cents." More likely, that person is motivated to peak performance by the company's mission that emphasizes the contribution of technology to advance science and people's welfare.

Sure there are company founders whose primary ambition is to score in the instant multimillionaire-making IPO sweepstakes. Instead of building a great company of enduring value, their ambition is to come up with a big idea that can be taken public or get acquired in 12 to 18 months. But the true spirit of the garage is about working to leave a legacy. It's about working with the field's best and brightest to get a sublime product out the door. Inspirational missions put something worthwhile at stake every business day, not just the day of the IPO.

The link between an organization's core purpose, its corporate culture, and its ability to procure top talent is widely underestimated. Even if senior management places "profit maximization" as a chief priority, the means of securing the talent to deliver on that objective depends on fostering a compelling work environment. A strong financial package is a powerful motivator, but growing numbers of employees are looking for rewards for the wallet and the soul.

Trendsetting companies realize their people draw from a heightened level of inspiration that comes from a mission or cause that goes beyond profit or getting rich. Without a transcendent mission, individuals will lack the courage and determination to pursue challenges and goals year after year.

Inspiring missions describe a contribution to be made to employees, customers, or the larger society. The inspiration comes from aligning with a cause that goes beyond self-interest, a cause that is truly noble. Listen to the causes of these trendsetting companies:

- **Timberland:** "To equip people to make their difference in the world."
- **Nordstrom:** "To respond to unreasonable customer requests."
- **Ritz Carlton:** "Ladies and gentlemen serving ladies and gentlemen."
- **Coca Cola:** "To put our product within arm's reach of desire."
- **Whole Foods:** "Contributing to the quality of life renaissance."
- **Amazon.com:** "To be the world's most customer-centered company."

- **Johnsonville Sausage:** "To be the best place to work for people who will accept nothing less than greatness."
- **3M:** "The perpetual quest to solve unsolved problems innovatively."
- **Charles Schwab:** "Custodians of our customers' financial dreams."

When you read these company statements consecutively, the resounding theme is work that makes a difference. Inspiring missions speak to the higher ground of individual motivation; the chance to create a worthwhile destiny and leave a legacy through the process of work itself.

Self-scrutinizing questions

1. When top talent prospects ask why they should work for you, how else can you reply besides, "The job pays well and we have great stock options?"
2. While not reflected in your turnover rates, how many of your people have left the company emotionally because of its humdrum mission or lackluster strategy?
3. What methods can you employ to repeatedly engage your team in acknowledging, reflecting on, or re-examining your purpose for being in business (besides making a profit)?

Core value #3: Autonomy

Why aren't people more committed to their companies' goals? This question perplexes plenty of executives in bureaucratic organizations. While it is easy to point to bad hiring decisions, or complain that empowerment is overrated as a management technique, the best place to look for an answer is in the mirror. The unflattering truth is that button-down bureaucratic practices usurp people's capacity for commitment.

By design, bureaucracies allocate decision-making power to an elite few. The organization's lower echelon become dependent on senior management to call the shots that shape their collective destiny. Why should they offer their discretionary energy to projects when their hands are tied and their minds are set on a just-follow-orders mode? How can people feel committed when they are offered a sliver of responsibility for the way things turn out?

Trendsetters recognize the folly of imposing tight controls on decision-making in an organization that desires innovative thinking. Their stance on autonomy is based on the dictum: *Hire self-motivated people and give them a long leash.* They trust people to align their actions in a way that forwards the organization's goals.

A helpful way to think about the degree of freedom people have in crafting their work is the distinction between *role compliance* and *role pioneering*. In a role-compliant environment, job descriptions are passed down from generation to generation of jobholders, sometimes surviving for so long they could be considered historical documents. Role-compliant employees fit their actions to their job descriptions. Their role parameters remain in place even as market conditions change and the needs of internal and external customers are no longer being met.

In contrast, role pioneers break free of the shackles of a limiting job description. Rather than engaging in slavish compliance, they reinvent their jobs to anticipate the latent needs of customers. Role pioneers are responsible for the new roles that have emerged in business in recent decades including: executive coaches, personal fitness trainers, chief information officers, sports agents, and physician's assistants.

I once observed an amazing example of a role pioneer in action behind the fish counter at Quality Food Centers in Seattle, Washington. After the employee wrapped my fish, I gave him a little pop quiz by asking, "I realize certain species of fish are high in cholesterol and others are low. Can you tell me which ones are which?" He responded, "Sir, do you realize that there are two kinds of cholesterol?" and proceeded to give me a clear and authoritative medical explanation about high and low-density lipoproteins. I was witnessing the second coming of Marcus Welby! He then taught me several easy-to-prepare recipes for scallops and salmon. This seafood specialist even left his post behind the glass seafood case and briskly led me through the grocery aisles to pick out special spices and a cookbook.

How often have you received this treatment from your supermarket seafood department? Given the apparent restraints of the job, it is astounding to have a seafood specialist who approaches the standard of being the only one who does what he does.

In coaching clients on reinventing their roles, I provide a series of questions to get their imaginations working. Here's a sampling of those questions for you to use in your own efforts at role pioneering:

- What are the latent needs of your external and internal customers that no one seems to address? What role modifications or new roles might you design to take responsibility for solving those latent needs?

- What important projects or problems are being treated on a "we'll get around to it whenever time permits" basis, that need someone to take charge of? Design a role that gives you explicit responsibility for handling this problem that no one gets around to tackling.

- What is the issue your boss may be loosing sleep over? How might you contribute to resolving this issue?

- If you owned the business, how would you be performing your role?

- What accomplishment or performance level do you believe is extremely difficult to accomplish now with your current role restrictions but would become possible if your role could be changed?

- What are the technological changes your company is contemplating? What are the ways the expanded availability of quality information could be used to add value to your existing role?

The real power of role pioneering rests in its multiplier effect. In autonomous environments, one individual pioneering a role establishes new best practices and standards for peers to strive for, and in so doing, raises the bar for everyone. Eventually, the role being practiced doesn't resemble the role contained in the antiquated job description.

Role pioneers assume the freedom of authoring their own role within the parameters of organizational vision, goals, and values. The long-term effect of role pioneering in a company is the emergence of a cadre of team members who deliver value that exceeds the industry standard for their position.

In addition to role pioneering, another demonstration of autonomy is the degree and quality of employee empowerment. The Great Harvest Bread Company of Dillon Montana is a sterling example. The radical strategic assumption behind Great Harvest's franchising is a willingness to capitalize on the organizational creativity that flows when people are free to experiment. After a one-year apprenticeship where new franchisees learn established best practices, they are free to succeed or fail on their own judgment. Franchisees are not required to use the same promotions, paint stores the same colors, or even use the same bread recipes.

To maximize idea exchange, Great Harvest also encourages casual swapping of ideas and maintains formal systems to steer owners to their best sources of advice—fellow franchisees, not the "wisdom" of headquarters staff. Headquarters publishes quantitative reports including top 10 lists of the best performing bakers in 14 statistical categories, and a Numbers Club (joined by 85 percent of franchisees) where owners agree to open their books to the other 136 franchisees. Any franchisee can scour these reports to determine which of their fellow owners has mastered a particular aspect of the business or is in a similar situation and appears to have found better solutions to a problem.

The result of this level of franchisee autonomy at Great Harvest is a flow of new initiatives, best practices, and innovations that would be impossible in a replicator organizational environment.

Self-scrutinizing questions

1. What would happen if you invited people in your organization to rewrite their job descriptions to reflect their own creative ownership of the job? What response would you expect—dumbfounded silence, chaos, panic, or outbursts of joy?

2. How well have you attended to the full intricacies of organizational structures, incentives, and values in establishing a climate where empowerment can take hold?

3. Using the Great Harvest example, how can you encourage sharing of ideas within your organization or even members of your supply channel?

Core value #4: Nobility of mistakes

The trendsetter's quest to invent blockbuster products and services is not a zero defect process. Producing first-time-ever innovations is far different from continuously improving long-standing work processes. Companies that do not allow any mistakes can hardly expect their employees to go out on a limb with an idea that isn't tried and true.

In this spirit, Charles Schwab—the company that pioneered discount brokering, no-fee IRAs, and on-line trading—developed a culture that gave latitude for mistakes appropriate for pursuing leading edge innovation. The company's commitment to technological advances includes a long list of blunders since the 1980s including: Pocketerm and Schwab Quotes quotation services, Financial Independence money management software, and the Equalizer, an on-line transaction information device. Schwab interpreted the failed products as helpful given the company's mission to provide investors with the most useful and ethical brokerage services in America. Schwab does more than tolerate mistakes, it values mistakes using the phrase "noble failures." Mistakes are considered noble when they produce significant learning and conform to the following mistake-tolerance guidelines:

- The company can't be put at major risk.
- Reasonable precautions must be taken against failure. Do your homework. (Schwab is big on tracking consumer values and attitudes, gathering facts, financial modeling, and profit projection.)
- The organization will gain significant learning whether the innovation succeeds or fails.

- It is important to fail in small prototypes rather than in large-scale market tests.

The cumulative effect of Schwab's learning from failures produces innovations that anticipate the latent needs of the marketplace. Beyond the financial windfall that comes with being first, Charles Schwab noted that a culture that accepts and supports mistakes also entices top talent. He said,

> *"The fact that we were involved in these failures made people realize we were a place where innovation was going on, and that in turn attracted people who would help us move ahead. We became known as a place where people are not afraid to take chances."*

Self-scrutinizing questions

1. Have you articulated clear guidelines about the limits of failure tolerance similar to the Charles Schwab criteria? If not, what might they be?
2. Can you point to innovative experiments currently being undertaken in your business? If not, when was the last time someone stuck his or her neck out to do something wildly unconventional? How about moderately unconventional?
3. What happens in your culture when a mistake is made? Is the champion for the initiative that caused the undesirable outcome treated more like scum or nobility?
4. Do you have systematic methods in place to fully share the learning derived from a mistake?

Core value #5: Ad hoc innovation pockets

For companies that began in a garage, the spirit of innovation remains ingrained in the company culture as it grows—if it can succeed in developing an organizational structure that replicates the intense camaraderie and ownership of the product experienced by the team in the garage. At that time, there were no interdepartmental turf battles over who deserved credit for results. Survival was at stake. The company's destiny unfolded one heartbeat at a time until its initial product shipped.

How can you duplicate in a big company the conditions conducive to the creative connections that existed in the garage? Most creativity pacesetters bypass hierarchy in favor of "ad hoc innovations pockets." "Ad hoc" refers to team formation on an as-needed basis, with members disbanding when a project is completed. These pockets are free from rigid departmental and hierarchical affiliation so the right talent is able to bring their expertise and perspective to a project.

To foster the conditions expressed in these pockets of innovation you will need to:

- *Develop perspective-rich work teams.* The wording is important here. The familiar business jargon of "interdisciplinary" and "cross functional" work teams doesn't adequately reflect the range of perspective required to stimulate innovation. Since divergent perspectives are essential in the early creative process, innovation is best accomplished by bringing together people with different academic training, work experience, professional affiliations, proximity to customers, and generational and cultural affiliations.

- *Elicit the input of outsiders.* At appropriate times, it is necessary to actively include the viewpoints of customers, wholesalers, suppliers, and strategic alliance members.

- *Play the best players available.* In sports, a coach wouldn't think of resting the team's superstars on the bench during a championship game. When the stakes are high, you play the best players available. The rule is the same for trendsetters: elite people work on elite projects. Why confine top talent to a business running on autopilot where their contribution is slight, when they could be participating in a newly conceived venture with incredible upside potential? Departmental affiliation takes a back seat to penetrating potentially golden opportunities.

- *Mix and match to achieve the right group chemistry.* Divergent perspectives are only a starting point. Managers must balance team diversity with supportiveness. Supportiveness includes features like: shared excitement for the team's goal; willingness to help teammates through setbacks and difficult periods; and respect for the unique knowledge and perspective that other members bring to the table. Supportive fit among team members combined with a diverse array of talent produces the ideal combination for sparking creative endeavor.

- *Allocate time for creative thinking.* A sad but true fact for the time-conscious businessperson: Creativity takes time. Many busy work teams settle for the best idea arising out of a brisk brainstorming session and then move on to whatever is next on the to-do list. Unfortunately, brainstorming largely surfaces ideas people already have contemplated, not the ingenious ones that come from unexpected connections of ideas. Original thinking is the product of holding out for better solutions, looking at problems from different vantage points, mixing knowledge from different fields, using disagreements to shake up entrenched positions, and allowing incubation time for creative ideas to emerge.

- *Honor creative dissent.* Intel is famous for its use of conflict as part of its self-questioning culture. Would-be innovators do not present their ideas before an assembly of polite yes-men. They must face a barrage of intense grilling and savagely frank feedback. While the ensuing conflict is blunt and at times brutal, Intel team members learn to disagree without being disagreeable. By allowing their people to air strongly held differences, Intel believes the eventual solutions are likely to be of better quality. The group norm of harnessing contention to reach consensus on a quality idea opposes the tendency to settle for a watered-down compromise to preserve the peace.

- *Share great ideas.* Can we really afford to throw up our hands in concession to hectic circumstances to explain the lack of cross-functional conversation and intellectual isolation? What is the opportunity cost in terms of connections that stimulate creativity? Barbara Waugh, Worldwide Personnel Manager of

HP Labs WBIRL (World's Best Industry Research Laboratory) program, took small steps in the process of transformative change by facilitating people talking to each other. She organized informal Friday afternoon talks to discuss whatever technological issues happened to be on people's minds, and regularly drew between 50 and 150 participants.

Self-scrutinizing questions

1. What is the "solitary confinement factor" in your company? In other words, to what degree do people work on tightly bound departmental projects without a chance to share new ideas with colleagues working in a different functional silo?
2. How many projects are going on in your company where individuals from different departments are regularly collaborating? What practices can you develop to inform people about innovative projects being entertained throughout the company and ways they can nominate themselves to participate?
3. Are you comfortable leaving the interdepartmental exchange of knowledge up to chance meetings at the water fountain or coffeepot?
4. What simple ways can you devise to get people talking with each other to increase the likelihood of creative connections occurring?
5. When your people discover a practice that works, do they routinely think, "Who else can benefit from this learning?"
6. What communication vehicles can you offer your people to efficiently share their best practices company wide? Think of videotapes, e-mails, data banks, company wide voice mail messaging, or even site visits to see the new ideas being implemented.

Assessing Your Own Company's Spirit of the Garage

The following questions are for assessing how well your existing culture supports strategic innovation. Each question has two parts, a simple rating (circle the number) and a space for comments.

For best results, please answer these questions with "ruthless honesty." Compare your answers with other team members to notice the specific observations of culture that are reflected in your answers.

1. What percentage of your senior management team's time is spent on conversations about strategic thinking aimed at creating new business opportunities and new value for customers?

   <10%   10-20%   20-30%   30-40%   >40%

Comments: _____

_____

_____

_____

_____

2 Does your organization have a strategic plan in writing that establishes direction and priorities for at least 2-5 years ahead?

   No   1   2   3   4   5   Yes

Comments: _____

_____

_____

_____

_____

3. To what extent does your company have a formal strategic planning process that surfaces, develops, and supports innovation?

   No formal process   1   2   3   4   5   Formal process in place

Comments: _____

_____

_____

_____

_____

4. Do you have processes in place that encourages front line employees to offer customer insights and ideas for new business opportunities to senior management?

    No   1   2   3   4   5   Yes, a formal process

Comments: _____

_____

_____

_____

_____

5. Do senior executives have roles and responsibilities defined in such a way that they can prioritize sufficient time for working on strategic long-term issues as opposed to operational/ tactical issues?

    No   1   2   3   4   5   Yes

Comments: _____

_____

_____

_____

_____

6. What percentage of senior management's time is spent executing a prepared strategic plan (as contrasted to time spent putting out fires or reacting to customer requests)?

    <10%   10-20%   20-30%   30-40%   >40 %

Comments: _____

_____

_____

_____

_____

7. What percentage of time is spent in meetings with customers/
    key accounts discussing long-term strategic issues (as opposed
    to progress reviews and short term goal setting)?

    <10%   10-20%   20-30%   30-40%   >40%

Comments: _____
_____
_____
_____
_____

8. Does your company have any reward or recognition pro-
    grams explicitly tied to innovation (as opposed to process
    improvement suggestions)?

    No   1   2   3   4   5   Yes

Comments: _____
_____
_____
_____
_____

9. Is strong disagreement acceptable in your culture? Do con-
    versations tolerate no-holds-barred disagreement in the inter-
    est of improving innovations rather than settling for watered
    down compromises in the interest of being nice to one
    another?

Disagreement discouraged   1   2   3   4   5   Disagreement encouraged

Comments: _____
_____
_____
_____
_____

10. What percentage of time at your annual strategic planning retreat is typically spent on developing an original strategic position for the future (as opposed to reviewing last year's results, extrapolating goals based on recent numbers, etc)?

    <10%   10-20%   20-30%   30-40%   >40%

Comments: _____

_____

_____

_____

_____

11. Does your company use different methods for understanding the needs of tomorrow's customers (about 2-5 years ahead) compared to how you go about understanding the needs of today's customers?

    No   1   2   3   4   5   Yes

Comments: _____

_____

_____

_____

_____

12. Has an individual been assigned formal responsibility for managing your organization's innovation performance/results?

    No   1   2   3   4   5   Yes

Comments: _____

_____

_____

_____

_____

Off the Org Charts

Great strategies are worth no more than the paper they are printed on unless you have the organization to implement them. Now you know why so few companies become persistent trendsetters. Not every company is willing to seek out the best people, to inspire them with a task worth doing, to risk giving them autonomy and freedom to make mistakes, and to facilitate independent project teams. Not every company develops the kind of organization that can be the only one to do what it does. This is why developing the spirit of the garage pays off so profoundly both in net worth and self-worth.

Chapter

9

Strategic Planning
for Innovators

Chapter

Strategic Planning
for Innovators

*"The impetus for Microsoft's response to the Internet
didn't come from me or our senior executives.
It came from a small number of dedicated employees
who saw events unfolding."*

—Bill Gates, Microsoft Corporation

Strategies shape destinies. Yet strategic planning for innovation is the most misunderstood process in any business. While most companies spend a small fortune developing every detail of their one-year or five-year strategic plan, they scarcely bother to examine the *process* whereby they come up with that plan.

In trendsetting companies, strategic planning is a process, not a one-time event. It is dynamic, not static. And it involves all the people in the company, not just senior managers.

We can safely assume that most senior managers know the nuts and bolts of what goes into a strategic plan, which is fine. However, their planning process has probably remained unchanged for decades—so innovation occurs only by coincidence.

How do you rethink strategic planning so you produce bold innovations?

Now here is the critical issue. If the inherited planning process supports the level of innovation needed to compete today, you are lucky. In most cases, the process will favor replication. There is a huge difference between strategic planning that evolves to suit replication and one designed for strategic innovation.

Strategy plays too vital a role to tolerate planning processes that can't meet your trendsetter goals. So let's boil them down to essentials. If you can say yes to these four questions you are in great shape:

- Does your process increase the chances of conceiving a blockbuster idea?
- Can you repeat the process reliably?
- Does your strategic plan provide a sustainable competitive advantage?
- Does the plan inspire enthusiastic execution?

While the study of strategic planning for innovation is still incomplete, I have learned a great deal from observing how my trendsetter clients inject the seven Big Ideas into their planning processes. The following guidelines will help you rethink every part of your process for strategy development to capitalize on your organization's full capacity for innovation.

Guidelines for the Innovative Planner

Start with trendsetting aspirations

All your communications about the purpose of strategic planning should position innovation as the top priority. Be clear from the outset that fixing and improving take a back seat to finding ways to be the only company that does what you do.

Warning! In most companies, the need for bold innovation is hugely underestimated. Organizations have a number of built-in biases for maintaining the status quo. The bias for quick-fix, expedient solutions in order to get back to the real business of running the company disregards the time needed for conceiving original innovations. The bias to produce short-term results leads to conservative strategic moves and rules out developing new capabilities. Finally, the bias to play by the industry's rules of competition will put a damper on innovations that stray too far from what's customary and familiar.

Given these biases, leaders inevitably face a barrage of colleagues' reasons why current conditions are not conducive for innovation, such as cash flow problems, soft markets, the tight labor market, tightening of venture capital, or difficulty in gauging future trends. It may be tempting to cave in to their appeals to be reasonable, and thereby compromise the magnitude of innovation.

Be careful not to fall for misguided considerations that focus only on obvious short-term consequences, while ignoring the long-term impact of delaying innovation. A classic example is the tendency to put off innovation during a recession or bad business cycle. "Wait until the economy recovers," proclaim the innovation nay-sayers, who resort to reaching earnings forecasts by cutting costs and praying that the core product will produce sufficient sales. Trendsetting leaders don't take a "time out" from the pursuit of innovation and double-digit growth. Instead, they get innovative in both draining costs and seeking out less expensive sales growth opportunities. For instance, cost cutting could involve eliminating jobs that can be Web-enabled, locating cheaper means of product sourcing, or inventing more efficient, lower cost manufacturing processes. To increase revenues, they might create new sales and marketing positions, expand markets through joint ventures, or develop service contracts for products they and their competitors manufacture. These three moves boost today's sales, which in turn, become assets to support future innovation. The future isn't compromised even during a bad market cycle.

Put the world on your guest list

Given the importance of fresh eyes to spark innovation, it is a mistake to confine planning to the senior management team. Senior managers' thinking is often saturated with industry dogma, and they already have a good idea of one another's opinions on business issues. In fact, they are the ideal group to assemble if you want to crank out a "no-surprises" strategy. Business history contains notable occasions where new product ideas and opportunistic vision originated from the ranks below senior management.

Bill Gates, for instance, is reputed to have marvelous foresight about the future of technology, but he nearly missed the initial window of opportunity around the Internet. In 1993, Gates and his colleagues viewed the Internet as a network for academics and techies, and relegated it to a fifth or sixth strategic priority. Who turned Gates on to the potential of the Internet? No, it wasn't Al Gore. The inspiration came from university students and a number of newer, non-management employees at Microsoft. It started with Steve Sinofsky, Gates' technical assistant, who was blown away by how rapidly Cornell University's operations became saturated by Internet applications. He and younger Internet-savvy employees were able to rally everyone to the Internet cause. In describing how this came about, Gates said, "Their story exemplifies our policy, from Day One, that smart people anywhere in the company should have the power to drive an initiative."

Microsoft isn't alone in benefiting from democratizing its strategy process. During the Depression, Kraft attempted to market an inexpensive cheddar cheese powder that consumers refused to buy. A St. Louis sales rep, seeking a way to unload his inventory, added individual cheese powder packages to boxes of macaroni. Grocers sold the macaroni and cheese combo as a "Kraft Dinner" which soon became part of the company's product line.

A store manager in sunny Los Angeles submitted the idea for Starbucks' killer product, Frappaccino. If responsibility for innovation had been limited to managers based at headquarters in the northern climes of rainy Seattle, a chilled coffee-based product probably wouldn't exist.

To bring high levels of creativity to your strategic planning process, put some wild cards on your guest list. Involve newcomers to your business. Listen to people who have spent the bulk of their careers in other industries and business cultures. Include near-retirees who bring a tell-it-like-it-is frankness to exposing models that no longer work. Next, invite people from the field to share their in-the-trenches viewpoint. If you are a global company, seek input from business units outside of the country you are headquartered in.

Certainly such a large group would not be appropriate to participate at the annual strategic planning retreat. To involve diverse perspectives, organize a series of conversations about strategic topics. Invite people to sessions on such topics as: determining existing and needed core competencies, brainstorming new business opportunities, revealing the assumptions we take for granted (remember the observational comic exercise), or translating tracking trend information into latent needs of tomorrow's customers. To provide continuity and insure the senior management is kept in the communication loop, have a top-level executive participate in each of these conversations.

Expect to strategize every day, not every year

The notion of the annual planning retreat as the revered occasion to hammer out the strategy for the next two to five years is archaic. Put this bureaucratic sacred cow out to pasture for a couple of reasons. First, a once-a-year discussion will not produce original strategy. Innovations evolve from ongoing dialogue and percolating ideas. You don't just sit down in a day or two and come up with something brilliant.

The second reason is that the capacity for strategic and innovative thinking is like any skill—use it or lose it. If you don't train yourself to consistently view the business with fresh eyes, antiquated assumptions creep into decisions. Staying strategically sharp requires practice every day, not once a year.

Strategy is best seen as a work in progress. No matter how dazzling the plan seems on paper, or how effective the results in the marketplace, strategy should never be treated as a finished product. The annual strategic planning retreat shouldn't serve to originate new plans, but rather to crystallize hundreds of daily strategic conversations that occurred throughout the year. The retreat then leverages and focuses the wealth of insights gained from customers, suppliers, and an empowered work force. The key role of senior management is to decide which of the ideas should be incorporated into the strategic plan.

Focus on strategic health, not just financial health

Replicators focus on financial health. Their obsession about short-term measures of profits, cash flow, shareholder value, and growth rates causes two problems. First, financial health ignores valuable data contained in indices of strategic health. The second problem lies in how financial health information is interpreted. Replicators treat the hard data with numbers-don't-lie reverence. If the numbers look great, the reflexive response is not to mess with a good thing. If the numbers aren't up to expectations, they want to institute cosmetic tweaks to tidy up the P&L mess for the short term. Unintentionally, they trade off major long-term opportunities for today's better-looking balance sheets.

Financial health measures alone can instill a dangerous self-deception. Isolated from other considerations, how does anyone know whether a set of numbers signifies the peak performance of a company that will soon be headed down hill, or one that is only beginning a growth spurt that will soon make today's numbers seem wimpy?

The full picture on the state of any business must incorporate measures of many more factors than just financial. Measures of strategic health can point to potential crises years before they might occur. Constantios Markides, professor at London Business School, cited several indicators of strategic health in his book, *All the Right Moves*. These included:

- Changes in the industry and the company's capacity to deal with the new environment.
- Comparisons of financial health to that of top competitors.
- Customer loyalty.
- Customer satisfaction.
- Distributor and supplier feedback.
- Employee morale.
- Employee turnover.
- Market share.
- New products in the pipeline and innovative projects undertaken.
- Quality of the management team.
- Strength of the company culture.

When you issue business reports, start monitoring these measures of strategic health, and get the numbers that will support planning for sustained competitive advantage.

Avoid direct competition; discover minimally contested markets

Replicators use competitive information to improve their competence in jumping on the industry bandwagon. When asked why such scrutiny is paid to following where the industry is heading, the stock answer is "to remain competitive." What sounds like a reasonable decision is actually an admission of being behind the competition, needing to catch up, and committing to being a follower. Copycats are abdicating responsibility for doing their own original strategic thinking. But a more basic issue still has to be addressed. For starters, whom do you define as a competitor? The most dangerous competition may not even be attending your trade association's annual meeting. How important is competitive analysis when you can't keep close tabs on non-traditional players who have a clear shot at making an end run on your customers? What is your defense from intruders that introduce novel and potentially threatening business models?

Clayton Christiansen, author of *The Innovator's Dilemma,* describes a frequent pattern of market leaders being overthrown by hard-to-detect competitors, who introduce "disruptive technologies" which originate in less profitable, emerging markets, which eventually become more lucrative than mainstream market. Digital photography is replacing photographic film, self-adjusting glasses are replacing traditional prescription lenses, e-mail is replacing phone communication or express mail deliveries.

Rather than taking stock of where the competition is today, go where there is no competition or where you can bring new value that your competition can't match. In strategic innovation, trendsetting strategists systematically explore a broad range of potential customers, including such categories as:

- Customers whose needs fit our products but whom we're currently not serving.

- Customers who no competitor is serving well because there appear to be no cost effective solutions. Example: Progressive Insurance is targeting the high risk, more accident-prone driver.

- Customers who are experiencing compromises in some phase of the buyer experience cycle; purchase, delivery, usage, supplementary products and services, maintenance, and disposal. Example: Barnes & Noble is reinventing the book purchasing experience, by encouraging generous sampling of books and offering excellent reference services from trained staff.

- Customers who represent age ranges (e.g., seniors, children) who are not targeted by your competitors. Example: ESPN was the first all sports TV channel, and is now segmenting to ESPN Classic for the retro-Baby Boomers and senior citizens, and producing the X Games featuring extreme sports that appeal to teenagers and Generation X.

- Customers with new needs emerging because of changing business trends. Example: With more mergers, consulting firms are addressing the challenge of effectively assimilating different organizational cultures.

- Customers you currently serve who have customers with changing needs.

- Customers who may benefit from outsourcing business functions.

- Customers who have blind spots in their strategic plan and are not paying attention to threats or opportunities.

- Customers who would benefit from services that are usually associated with other industries.

- Customers in different geographic regions who could benefit from your services.

- Customers undergoing shifts in values. Example: Hotels are offering fitness centers and special cuisine menus for the increasing numbers of guests who've adopted wellness lifestyles.

- Customers who want the convenience of one-stop shopping solutions.
- Current customers who are buying your products and might also benefit from your core competencies. Example: GE is providing management consulting on six sigma quality and management development.
- Customers who are facing compromises from the services of several industries. Example: Home Depot's strategy recognizes that home improvement junkies have two unsatisfactory choices—paying large fees to remodelers to fix up their home or large amounts to small hardware stores for tools and materials. In addition, the do-it-yourself construction crowd often needs education to complete the repair or remodel.

Strategies that focus on seeking out minimally contested markets will help you sustain those record-breaking numbers for years instead of months. Why engage in intensive competition when you can create a window of opportunity when the market is yours for the taking?

Use research to get information on potential markets

Most market research does a fine job of measuring what traditional customers expect from an industry's product and service offering. If you want to anticipate the potential sales volume or likely market share for a product line extension, market research can provide those answers. However, most research says nothing about what buyers would want if dramatic new value became available. The studies also have little relevance in gauging the needs and responsiveness of emerging markets.

In strategic innovation, senior management adopts the intellectually honest position of admitting, "We don't know squat when it comes to accurately projecting market potential in emerging markets as with a dramatically new value offering."

Operating with an honest sense of uncertainty, management can take several constructive actions. First, they can give up the false safety net of relying on fuzzy and debatable financial projections. The simple assertion "the data doesn't suggest a market for this idea," no longer delivers an instantaneous thumbs-down to an idea.

Second, they design research to test hypothetical assumptions that suggest potential business opportunities.

There are two ideal spots for testing hypotheses. At the front end of strategic innovation, market research helps to understand the values, shopping patterns, and lifestyles of new customers. Later, at the point of field-testing, use research to study the reactions and concerns of early adopters of your innovation. Their responses often expose unanticipated customer concerns before they become magnified in larger segments of customers.

Adapt ideas from other industries

Replicators over-emphasize benchmarking against their own industry leaders. Careful judgment is needed here. Too often this type of benchmarking simply produces barely recognizable shades of differentiation on subtle quality measures rather than introducing original value to the market. Conventional benchmarking usually intensifies competition. When everyone's quality is strong, the customer doesn't see any difference, and where do you think the replicators compete on? Low price.

Trendsetters, on the other hand, capitalize on the full potential of benchmarking. They introduce new value to the marketplace by using world-class practitioners from outside their industries as reference points for raising the bar in their own. Nordstrom, for example, borrowed the idea of a concierge service from five-star hotels. Likewise, GE learned about asset management from Toyota, and modified quick marketing intelligence from the Wal-Mart model. Fed Ex applied the banking industry's method of clearing checks overnight through a central processing point into its hub-and spoke-concept where every package went to Memphis and then was flown to its final destination.

Benchmarking against other industries' best practices stirs your creative juices and suggests imaginative applications that offer distinctively new value to your customers.

Stir the imagination with scenario planning

Peter Schwartz in *The Art of the Long View* explained that scenario planning should not attempt to pick a preferred future and hope it comes to pass. Its purpose is to help an organization make sound strategic decisions for a range of plausible futures. This type of planning typically hones in on four major images of the future:

1. what is likely to happen,
2. a wild card,
3. the worst case situation, and
4. heaven on earth.

The most striking difference between scenario planning and strategic innovation lies in its intent. Scenario planning is reactive, threat-focused, and serves as a dress rehearsal for the future. This process helps an organization to be poised for action when the indicators of a particular future unfold.

In contrast, strategic innovation is proactive, opportunity-focused, exploits changes happening right now, with the intent of determining a strategically advantageous future. The objective is to orchestrate the steps to bring this preferred future into existence.

Within the total package of strategic innovation, scenario planning can be a wonderful tool for stirring imagination about potential forces of change and their impact on latent customer needs. Used properly, it should inject more creativity into your discussion of trends information, providing your organization with an original viewpoint about the future of your industry—ideally, one that surprises your competition.

Change the leadership team's thinking

So how do you determine whether a strategic planning exercise has been successful? The obvious indicator is that competitors struggle to duplicate the advantage you have developed. The second and less obvious measure of success is gauged by how much the leadership team's thinking has shifted, because any strategy is based on a set of assumptions about leadership, profit-making, and competitiveness. Consequently, special attention should be given to exposing these assumptions so they can be judged in each strategic planning cycle. In my strategic innovation consultations, clients keep a log of their foundational strategic assumptions. At the end of each day, the group shares their log entries, which are compiled on a flip chart. Here's a sampling of frequent foundational assumptions:

- "Don't get involved in capital intensive businesses."
- "We pursue high margin opportunities."
- "We will compete in markets only where we can be #1 or #2 in market share."
- "The more products a customer purchases, the greater the likelihood of retaining their business."
- "Focus on getting young consumers to increase the lifetime value of a customer."
- "When a strategy is easy to copy the margins will come down quickly as the competition follows the leader."
- "Borrow money for quick cash gains, not for long term capital intensive projects which should be drawn from core business cash flow."
- "Never trade control of strategy for public money."
- "Being an effective aggregator of other businesses is a valuable core competency."
- "The best way to grow margins is by reducing costs."
- "We aim to be both low cost and value-added—rather than one or the other."

One by one, each assumption is judged on the basis of which ones are still relevant, which to discard as no longer effective, and which to challenge by conceiving a business opportunity that contradicts the assumption. For instance, take the assumption, "We win by making acquisitions that produce economies of scale and volume buying advantages." Going in the opposite direction, the strategic planners might devise their business as a tiny niche player whose strengths lie in customizing offers to a targeted customer base. The exercise creates an understanding of competitors' strategies and also reveals vulnerabilities in the current strategic position.

By putting strategic assumptions up for critical examination, the senior management team stays conscious of the very thinking that guides their company's destiny. This exercise prevents taking assumptions for granted, and encourages willingness to explore new assumptions.

Besides strategic assumptions, other measures of changes in thinking would be noticing latent needs, distinguishing new core competencies, revealing previously unrecognized customer segments, noticing emergent industry trends, or developing new product and service ideas.

Dance with what you get

The final difference between strategic planning and strategic innovation is how the agreed-upon-plan gets implemented in the marketplace. This point in the process reveals stark differences between replicators and trendsetters.

Replicator strategists try to determine the exact objectives, to spell out the plan that has the strongest chance of accomplishing those objectives, and then to allocate the required resources. These planners most often adopt a "get it right the first time" approach to introducing product and service innovations.

Unfortunately, the strategies developed in the isolated tranquility of a management retreat don't always track with the quirky and unpredictable reactions of customers. Unanticipated changes derail even the most carefully considered strategic moves. Sooner rather than later, the plan on paper must be adjusted, calling increasingly upon the leader's creative instincts to navigate in an uncertain world.

Strategic innovation is based on understanding that innovation is not a zero defect process. Organizations must prepare for repeated course correction in response to customer feedback. Strategic innovation is part careful planning, and part trial and error until you hit upon what works. The first part of planning aims to discover a definite direction to move in to serve the marketplace. The second part is learning to "dance" with changing conditions.

"Dancing" is the experimentation that transpires when hypothetical strategic plans interact with the dynamic marketplace. The steps to the dance are simple. Strut forward into the marketplace by placing your innovation prototype within reach of potential users in early field tests. Step back and observe customer reactions, inquire after feedback, and dig for every possible insight. Scan the business environment for any ripple effects your innovation exerted in the marketplace. Swing out one more time using what you have now learned, to deliver a refined value offering. Keep swinging in and out until you get it right.

Notice the make-it-up-as-you-go tempo. Strategic innovation is messy. More time is spent in making mistakes and learning from them, than in trying to produce perfect plans. The resulting plan is not an ironclad irreversible set of moves but rather a commitment to a strategic direction. Repeated course correction is the modus operandi. The introduction of each prototype or product version stimulates customer feedback, which in turn ushers in a whole new set of questions, dilemmas, and choices. The trendsetter's job is to dance with them.

Sequence your thinking

One of the greatest challenges to successful innovation is the ability of a team of planners to orchestrate their thinking in a sequence that produces maximum results. Unfortunately, most strategic processes aren't analyzed in terms of their "thinking requirements" so innovation bogs down and people become frustrated.

Innovation suffers when planning groups fall into three classic patterns. Some groups may become so enthralled with generating ideas, and underplay the need to rigorously gather facts about the marketplace, and end up with half-baked ideas. Other planning teams become overly analytic and always crave additional information before they can reach a decision, often missing the window of opportunity. The third common failure is when strategists judge ideas prematurely, so there's insufficient time for incubating enough new ideas.

The best strategic planning teams deliberately orchestrate their thinking to correlate with the mental tasks at hand. In broad terms, strategic innovation involves three major thinking tasks: idea generation, information gathering and decision-making, and formulating short and long-term objectives and action plans.

In the early stages of strategic innovation, the paramount task is to generate original ideas. The focus of thinking is on determining latent needs, synthesizing future trends, adapting other industries' innovations, and viewing the business with the various forms of fresh eyes. Much of the information in Chapters 4–6 describes this brand of thinking that generates out-of-the-box ideas.

The next stage of innovation involves more information gathering aimed at enhancing the quality of decisions. The planning team must prioritize their top criteria for judging business proposals. Common decision criteria include:

1. How well does the idea create a point of differentiation that is difficult for competitors to copy?
2. What is the potential for high margins?
3. What is the potential for significant organizational learning?
4. How well are we positioned in the supply chain to influence outcomes?
5. How can we employ the idea to maximize our strengths?
6. How can we employ the idea to minimize our weakness?
7. Does the idea capitalize on a powerful trend that will impact the industry's future?
8. Does the idea introduce new value to the marketplace?
9. How long will it take for the idea to produce positive cash flow?
10. Does the idea leverage our current capabilities or require new ones?
11. Is there significant emotional support for the idea?
12. What resources does the idea require and how will the resource drain effect other existing initiatives?

13. Is the idea an extension of our current products and services or does it place us in a position of having to acquire new customers, learn a different industry's operational practices, or build new business relationships?

14. Does the idea offer opportunity to develop strategic alliances that could become even more valuable in the future?

15. How can the idea improve brand equity?

16. What are the risks inherent in the idea? What risks are tolerable and intolerable?

17. How does the idea address a customer demand or expressed need?

Answering these questions will require researching to get relevant facts, weighing decision criteria to determine their relative influence, and ultimately committing to one or several innovations to implement.

The final phase of strategizing emphasizes strategic thinking for developing an integrated plan of action. If the strategy contains significant innovation, a large gap will exist between where the organization is today and where it intends to be in five years. Closing the gap calls for plotting a sequence of strategic milestones to be achieved year by year. The strategists must work from a desired strategic position five years ahead, and then going backward to define where the organization intends to be four years from now, then three years out, two years out, and finally the current annual plan. These strategic milestones can include objectives like expanding from a regional business to providing national coverage, enlarging specific core competencies by forming strategic alliances, rejuvenating the product line, reducing product development time by 75 percent, creating a new business division that leverages existing core competencies, or mastering technology that enables real time communication between headquarters and field based personnel. The plan of action phase of strategy demands thinking that weighs resources against aspirations, and operationalizes long-term objectives into a logical sequence of milestones building upon one another.

In simplified summary, the basic flow of strategic innovation moves from emphasis on idea generation, to analysis and information gathering mixed with decision-making, to the final concentration estimating resources and envisioning a logical plan of action. By understanding this basic flow a team of strategists stays on track so that the type of thinking required matches the task being undertaken at each phase of the planning process.

Case Examples of Strategic Innovation

Developing the next generation of innovative leaders

CROSSMARK describes itself as a "business service company." It provides sales, merchandising, marketing, consulting and outsourced management services to the business community, with particular emphasis on the consumer packaged goods industry. CROSSMARK, with headquarters in Plano, Texas, employs more than 9,000 associates in 61 offices throughout the United States, Canada and Australia.

Many industry supply channels engage in an active debate regarding which of the "middle men," (wholesale distributors, brokers) who don't directly manufacture or sell a product to consumers, should be eliminated to improve efficiencies. Manufacturers outsource their sales force and retailers outsource their distribution (rather than be self-distributing) largely to achieve cost savings.

John Thompson, President of the CROSSMARK Performance Group business, believes that being in the middle of the supply channel actually offers a unique opportunity for making valuable contributions to an entire industry. "Businesses select hard problems when they outsource. Every day, we are in a privileged position to learn a lot about what makes the consumer package industry run." Performance group specializes in innovation in solving complex problems that result from the increasing interdependence of B2B companies.

"If a problem is really hard, it means you don't have the right vantage point to look at it," says Thompson. The Performance Group targets business processes end to end, and brings together members of the supply chain, each specialists in their core competence, to come up with new mutually beneficial solutions. Rather than settling for a marginal role in the supply channel, CROSSMARK Performance Group produces solutions that no supply chain members could conceive or execute by themselves. The Performance Group approach emphasizing collaboration, coordination, and communication is practiced by all of the CROSSMARK business.

Chairman/CEO Butch Smith, a Winner of the Ernst & Young Entrepreneur of the Year Award in 2001, measures the true value of a leader as one who develops the most leaders rather than someone who commands the most followers. Consequently, CROSSMARK's strategic planning process is one that develops innovative thinking among its cadre of leaders. CROSSMARK's top tier of leaders are the eight members of the Management Advisory Council (MAC), which includes the presidents of the various businesses and other key executives, a portion of whom serve on a rotating basis. Smith begins the strategic planning cycle by appointing a strategic task force, a select group of managers from outside the MAC. The eight-member task force, with an appointed team leader, is charged with coming up with out-of-the box revenue generating opportunities that would capitalize on CROSSMARK's existing competencies. They are given three months to develop the ideas for presentation to the MAC.

In the initial task force meetings, the focus is on pure idea-generation with no judgment permitted. By the third meeting, ideas are evaluated with a careful analysis of pros and cons, and to determine which ones stirred up the group's enthusiasm. Which ideas provide the greatest differentiation and will be difficult for the competition to copy? How fast will an idea generate positive cash flow, higher profit margins? If the idea requires approaching new markets, what are the barriers to entry? What competencies would we have to develop or gain through making an acquisition or strategic alliance? Once seven top ideas emerged, a single individual chooses to be champion for the idea, and then begins research and analysis. The task force's favorite sources of information include Internet search engines, *Financial Times, Wall Street Journal, Hoovers,* and subscription services, which in turn, suggest relevant books or people to consult.

Wanting to insure all the key bases of analysis are covered, Butch Smith gives the task force a consistent format to guide their development of business opportunities. The format, borrowed from an approach originally developed by Xerox and popularized by Procter & Gamble, includes these components summarized in the acronym "SIERA":

S   Summarize the business environment that suggests the value of your idea, including demographic trends, the condition of the supply channel, statistics on customer buying patterns, competitive analysis, patterns in industry news events, specific strategic moves and public statements of competitors and customers, learnings from global markets facing similar issues, and projected sales figures.

I   State the proposed idea succinctly. In one or two sentences, describe a new product, service, business model, or market to penetrate, along with the new value being offered to customers and benefits to CROSSMARK.

E   Explain how the idea works with a conceptual overview of a plan of action. This explanation might include a proposed rethinking of the organizational chart, new services offered, outsourcing plans, opportunities for pilot testing, proposed acquisitions or strategic alliances, reinventing current roles to add value, and challenges in executing the idea.

R   Reinforce the key benefits to CROSSMARK. Benefits might include the potential for capitalizing or extending current capabilities, impact on reputation, chance to improve profit margins, opportunity for expansion into new minimally contested markets or deeper penetration of existing accounts, or likely return on investment.

A   Ask for the resources needed to execute the specific actions required.

The seven idea champions bring their analysis back to the task force for another round of critical review and rehearsing presentations.

At the MAC meeting, each idea is presented in about 45 minutes, with time allotted for feedback from the MAC members. From the viewpoint of senior management appraising business plans, they pose questions and share their assessments coving areas like:

- What are the fundamental assumptions underpinning the idea? Are they based on fact or opinion? Are the conclusions being drawn from assumptions logical? What other conclusions might be made?
- What are the areas of analysis that require more thorough research? Where are the blind spots where questions aren't being asked and where solid answers are needed?
- How can we take a good idea and expand the revenue generating potential?
- How can the idea serve as an opportunity to expand learning or develop core competencies and key strategic relationships?
- What are the implementation challenges inherent in a given idea?

The input from the MAC members helps to improve the strategic thinking of the task force members.

Ultimately, CROSSMARK's top shareholders, Butch Smith and David Baxley, Chief Operating Officer, review the seven proposed ideas and then bring their overall strategic plan back to another MAC meeting for their reactions and fine tuning.

While most companies are content coming up with a solid business plan, CROSSMARK's strategic innovation process is designed with purpose of continuous leadership development. Butch Smith is relentless in keeping high visibility on the planning process so a consistent approach is maintained and its ongoing effectiveness can be examined. With each successive planning cycle, the number of CROSSMARK managers who can contribute to high quality strategic conversation is enlarged. With the expansion of brainpower, it's no wonder CROSSMARK is recognized by its supply channel partners as an innovation engine.

The Office of the Future

Executing strategic innovation demands being ahead of the competition in anticipating the needs of tomorrow's customers. Yet so few companies invest in the resources that permit sustained effort to understand future trends and their implications.

The Ken Blanchard Companies is remarkable in its ability to face the truth and then take action on what they learn. Based in Escondido, California with international subsidiaries, The Ken Blanchard Companies is a full-service management consulting and training company with 250 employees.

In 1997, one of the co-founders, Dr. Margie Blanchard, stepped down from her role as President of Blanchard for ten years and created an Office of the Future for the firm. Despite all the rhetoric about the importance of future planning and being proactive, Dr. Blanchard recognized that the pressure in most organizations is to deliver on this quarter's or this year's results. This put the vital priority of preparing for the future in the "back seat," at Blanchard as well as among the firm's many clients.

Dr. Blanchard believes that people are naturally attracted to different types of activities. Some people relish the chance to continuously improve today's existing practices. They like to solve problems and upgrade work processes, and feel profound satisfaction in producing results. Other people love to contemplate the future and exert influence on how tomorrow will turn out. Future-oriented thinkers enjoy reflection, brainstorming, blue-sky thinking, and being freed up from the demands to get immediate results. Trying to force people to engage in work that departs from their natural preferences is often frustrating and unproductive.

The Office of the Future solves these problems by assembling a team that relishes working on the future and the firm funds their time to positively impact their company's destiny. Five staff members (4 on part-time status) serve as a primary think tank and nursery for new ideas, assisted by periodic collaboration with a 20 member Steering Committee. The purpose of this unit is to challenge the company's status quo and be a catalyst for needed change to insure a successful future. Consequently, they track and study trends, educate company leaders and strategic planners, and experiment with new ideas in their workplace.

How does the Office of the Future work? Now in its fourth year of operation, the inner circle is currently comprised of Dr. Blanchard, the corporate librarian, a consultant, a researcher, and a technology expert, who meet on a weekly or biweekly basis. Each spring, they meet with the Steering Committee to decide what areas to study, selecting topics like knowledge management, categorization of data, enterprise resource planning, leadership in 2008, Generation X and the new work force, the Internet economy, new ways of learning, virtual reality, and spirit at work. With a sharp focus to guide their inquiry, team members do research, attend conferences, share book reports, and interview clients. Each fall, the team for the Office of the Future conducts a two-day symposium for the executive team and other leaders whose areas of responsibility will be impacted by what they have studied and learned that year. White papers are shared, implications are discussed, and in some cases, follow up is transferred to new owners of a study area.

The work of the Office of the Future influences the content of marketing plans and new product development. Even more important, The Ken Blanchard Companies has a designated place for people to bring their innovative ideas in order to expand their potential value and strategize for their implementation. In turn, the Office of the Future shakes up status quo thinking. Margie Blanchard writes a series of future scenarios in the company newsletter to stir up lively conversations about distant possibilities. One scenario depicts a "Blanchard-Certified Manager" program, incorporating the use of the Internet to create lifelong relations with individual clients (rather than human resource departments) and to stay in communication as people move from company to company. The Office of the Future staff engages different departments in conversations about how technology can help improve their customer's experience. As an example, one percolating idea is to develop a Blanchard consultant's database where the key learnings from each client contact are recorded and made available to the entire consulting team.

The Office of the Future demonstrates "walking the talk" of enlightened leadership. The Ken Blanchard Companies dispenses with issuing platitudes about the importance of preparing for the future. Instead, they invest time and money, and assigned proper authority to an Office of the Future to insure that priority is given to preparing for the future.

Rethinking Strategic Planning to Emphasize Innovation

Figure 9.1 summarizes how the strategic planning process is transformed when innovation is top priority.

Figure 9.1
Rethinking strategic planning to emphasize innovation

From	To
Strategic planning as extrapolation.	Strategic innovation as revolution.
Market research to justify decisions.	Research to understand new customers.
Benchmark within industry.	Benchmark outside industry.
Competitive analysis to follow leaders.	Analysis to suggest new markets.
Land strategy with both feet planted.	Dance with unknown changes.
Strategic plan as annual ritual.	Strategy as unfinished product.
Strategy as domain of executive elite.	Democratization of strategy.
Attention largely to financial health.	Focus on financial and strategic health.

Both trendsetter and replicator companies engage in strategy development. The difference is that trendsetters use planning processes that look forward rather than backward, and that open the doors to opportunity. Strategic planning for innovation helps you unleash the entrepreneurial freedom to be the only ones to offer your value in the marketplace.

Epilogue

Unleashing
Entrepreneurial Freedom

Epilogue

Unleashing Entrepreneurial Freedom

"We cannot play with our destinies. As in chess, if you have a chance in life, you cannot tease it. You go for it."

—Soviet Chess Grandmaster Gary Kasparov

No human being can escape from freedom of choice. You choose until your last breath.

You are never free *not* to choose. Whether you act out of conformity or originality, both express your freedom. When you choose to conform to automatic routines or to allow budget debates to water down bold ideas—those are valid choices. When you choose to adopt new priorities or to sell a new business concept in the face of massive opposition—those are equally valid choices.

Even though all choices are valid, you may not have the power to exercise your full range of choice. The Fatal Assumption may be limiting your choices to replicating the past. If you master the Seven Big Ideas, however, you can exercise your full capacity for entrepreneurial freedom by developing your:

- Freedom to deliver distinctive value that addresses customers' latent needs.
- Freedom to entertain provocative, unresolved questions rarely contemplated in your industry.
- Freedom to design strategies that flaunt conventional wisdom.
- Freedom to create a culture that nourishes exceptional performance.

- Freedom to view your business from original perspectives.
- Freedom to maximize innovativeness by rethinking your strategic processes.

After you finish reading this book, how will you choose to use your entrepreneurial freedom?

A Heroic Choice

Every time I interview trendsetters in their offices, factories and stores, their original thinking captivates me. When I pepper them with questions like, "Where did you get that idea? Do you realize most of your colleagues consider it crazy?" their faces light up as if they had found an empathic friend or kindred rebel who appreciated how they had expressed their vision.

Although I enjoy seeing the innovations, I am in awe of the inner heroic quality that underlies such accomplishments. Brainstorming novel ideas is one thing. Executing them in an ultra-competitive marketplace is much more. It takes unusual courage.

For example, people on the trendsetter path struggle with fear and doubt. One new leader told me, "I'm scared that if I do anything innovative, I'll destroy the family business that's been passed down from generation to generation. What if everything goes down the tubes on my watch?" How did he resolve this fear? "Win or lose, I'd rather the outcome depend on calling my own shots," he decided. Taking a stand for self-expression is heroic.

Fear is usually accompanied by doubt. For example, in my own business, whenever I am at the brink of innovating, I feel enormous doubt because everything in the plan is so uncertain. Am I capable of out-thinking my competition? Am I targeting a latent need before the market recognizes the need? How will this change affect my established network of customers? Can I accomplish the personal growth required to reinvent myself? Where do I find the money? Where do I find the time to do it all? Every minute I spend on the future is another minute I am not producing income to improve this month's bottom line. Every minute I work on generating business for next month is another minute not invested in preparing for the future.

I am sure you can relate to the emotional turmoil described in this experience. At times I want to say, "Enough. Life will be easier if I lower my aspirations." And in that moment, my destiny hangs in the balance. For me, resolution comes when I recognize that grappling with fear and doubt will always be part of my process of innovation. You may face similar struggles as you engage in the freedom to innovate.

When fear and doubt enter, it is helpful to remember that the truth does set you free. You have to start with the truth that there are no risk-free routes to extraordinary accomplishments. The Marines say it more simply, "No guts, no glory."

Fear and doubt actually signal that you're up to something big.

The Ultimate "So What"

So what if your business becomes a trendsetter in its marketplace or succumbs to a slow demise! So what! Businesses rise and fall every day.

To reveal the ultimate "so what," let's return to the question, "How will you choose to use your entrepreneurial freedom?" Only let's look at this question on a larger scale. A national scale. What if entrepreneurial freedom is an expression of the personal freedom we are granted in the United States, which is the innovation catalyst for the concept of freedom in the world?

America's Founding Fathers laid the legal and inspirational groundwork for the thousands of trendsetters who have followed them. They introduced the concept of government by the people and for the people at a time when government was organized around the principle of divine rights for only a few people—kings and royalty. What an enormous gift! Americans live in a culture that makes it a right to pursue happiness. For some people, pursuing happiness is the dream of developing a business that expresses their talents and passionate values.

Without this legacy of freedom and the people who exercised it from our early history, trendsetting advances would not be nudging the world today. There'd be no next-day mail delivery. No total quality breakthroughs. No Internet revolution and e-commerce. No curing of infectious diseases. No Disneyland. No far-fetched dreams.

While business needs freedom, the reverse is also true—freedom needs business. We have a choice of how we treat freedom—as an entitlement that comes with being an American citizen or as a gift that requires constant practice. Trendsetting businesses are a training ground for the practice of entrepreneurial freedom, which has ripple effects in people's practice of freedom outside of work.

Imagine organizations where the Seven Big Ideas are reliably practiced. Teams would declare futures that bore little resemblance to the past. They would take stands on issues rather than seeking a watered-down consensus. They would view their customers' situations with fresh eyes. They would design cultures where opportunities for innovation were always being developed. And the influence of these trendsetting cultures would extend to employees' families who could raise children with a sky's-the-limit upbringing.

If business, even more than government, religion, and media, is the most influential institution, then the strategy and organizational environment of every trendsetting business comes with high stakes.

Business—to the degree it propagates entrepreneurial freedom—is at the center of the deepest and most important struggle in the world today.

Index

Index

About the Author

Art Turock is a leading resource in helping companies employ methods of strategic innovation to achieve a sustainable competitive advantage.

His ideas have empowered over one hundred Fortune 500 companies, including such clients as IBM, 3M, AT&T, Merck, as well as the Young Presidents' Organization. Turock's work has been featured in *USA Today, Success Magazine, Association Management*, and *The One Minute Manager* audiotape series. He is the author of the book, *Getting Physical: How to Stick with Your Exercise Program.*

Always in search of fresh perspectives, Turock conducts hundreds of site visits and executive interviews each year, producing a rich interaction with business mavericks and thought leaders. His thought provoking content, high energy, and extraordinary ability to customize his speeches gives audiences both entertainment and take-home value. Besides speeches, he facilitates strategic innovation consultations to empower progressive companies to rethink their strategic position and revamp their current strategy development process to generate original business opportunities.

Art Turock lives with his wife Haley in Kirkland, Washington.

For more information, contact:

Art Turock & Associates

11534 Holmes Point Drive NE

Kirkland, WA 98034